Michael J. Buchele, M.D.

PRACTICAL
WORK
ON
SELF

E J GOLD

GATEWAYS/IDHHB, INC. PUBLISHERS

Cover Art: An original woodcut by Paul Donner Spencer taken after a 1964 pen and ink drawing entitled "Man" by E.J. Gold.

Frontispiece photo by Philip Stark, NYC

Published by:
GATEWAYS / IDHHB, INC.
PO Box 370
Nevada City, CA 95959
(800) 869-0658, (916) 477-1116

Library of Congress Cataloging-in-Publication Data
Gold, E.J.
    Practical work on self / E.J. Gold.
        p. cm.
    Includes index.
    ISBN 0-89556-081-X — ISBN 0-89556-056-9 (pbk.) : $12.50
    1. Self-actualization (Psychology) 2. Self-control.
3. Spiritual life. 4. Self-actualization (Psychology)—Problems, exercises, etc. 5. Self-control—Problems, exercises, etc.
6. Spiritual life—Problems, exercises, etc. I. Title.
BF637.S4G64 1989
131—dc19   89-1377
                                                          CIP

TABLE OF CONTENTS

PREFACE

It's a bright, glaring spring day in Tucson, Arizona, 1973. I park my graduate student's red Ford Falcon in front of the Baskin-Robbins ice cream parlor and walk halfway down the block to my favorite second-hand bookstore. Inside, assailed by the familiar musty smell of dust and aging books, I head straight for the oriental religion and esoterica section, to see if there are any new arrivals.

Eureka! Next to the usual dingy copies of the *I-Ching*, dog-eared *Be Here Now*'s, cast off Alice Bailey books, there's a hardcover copy of *The Strange Life of Ivan Osokin*. It's a U.S. first edition. I've heard of this book but never read it. I thumb through the greyed pages, wondering who cut this loose from what sort of book collection in this Southern Arizona university town.

Some time later, sitting over coffee after a family dinner with an acquaintance who works as a technical editor for a large corporation, I listen to two teenagers talking about their *déjà vu* experiences. I find myself holding forth on Ouspensky's fiction and his unique elucidation of the *déjà vu* phenomenon. The teenage boy listens attentively, writes down the name of the novel, which I realize he will have trouble finding anywhere. The parents have no comment, look askance from one of us to the other over the rims of china coffee cups.

As I look back fifteen years—the span of one, maybe two generations since my university days—I realize that the culture has already encapsulated that moment of social history and moved swiftly ahead. In the late eighties atmosphere (a recurrence or recycling of turn-of-the-century and twenties' occult crazes) of wholistic expos, therapeutic shamanism, fire-walking, brain-wave manipulating machines, and in the words of Dan Millman "celebrity enlightenment manuals," it's difficult to call up the mood and ambience of that time when the search for practical esoteric ideas was a scavenger hunt, an adventure in penetrating the mysteries.

In those days a few of us passed around copies of de Ropp's *The Master Game* and Ouspensky's *In Search of the Miraculous,* trying to figure out how to do the exercises. We followed the tracks of monks and yogis and mystics through the Kabbalah, the *Philokalia* and Chuang Tze, Thomas Merton, Idries Shah, Carlos Castaneda (not at all a popular author with my acquaintances among the Yaqui tribe...), and *The Cloud of Unknowing.* We meditated in the desert by moonlight and checked out every obscure or apparently secret group that met to share hidden knowledge.

In that heady atmosphere, I answered an ad in an underground paper (another artifact of the era...) for a Gurdjieff-Ouspensky / esoteric discussion group. The intrepid sponsor of that circle, a barely articulate musician younger than I who seemed to me at first glance to be a full initiate, was in fact a former apprentice of E.J. Gold. In this context I first encountered Gold's writings and his particular formulation of the ideas of "work on self."

Gold himself describes in snapshot style his own earliest encounter with "the hidden guides," for him in New York City in the mid fifties, in *Visions in the Stone*. It's hard for me to say now whether the aura of mystery and the synchronicity of my experiences, and those of other "post-war babies," were more attributable to the spirit of the times—some grand grim reaper striding the land and piercing us with a scythe—or to our own desperate need for initiation into something besides the economic competence of contemporary adulthood. It doesn't truly matter, since the result was the same: false paths, disaster, oblivion for many, while for some a gateway to real work on self.

Following the thread I had been handed, I read Gold's *American Book of the Dead*, and numerous essays and pamphlets, all of which struck a deep nerve in me with their irony, humor, penetrating insight into consciousness, and unremitting, Twainian critique of contemporary life. Above all, compared to most literature of the esoteric book section and the university library, E.J. Gold's works offered an accurate description and diagnosis of the moribund condition of the "three-brained beings of planet earth" (that is, the beings with mental, emotional, and moving centrums), and something more. They provided an accessible *practice,* the beginnings of a remedy through exercises given with lucid instructions, without arcane symbolism, occult paraphernalia or elaborate overlay of philosophical beliefs.

When eventually I made my way to California to meet E.J. Gold for the first time, I realized that he was simply being true to his nature and his aims to present the ideas as he did; the Work that he proposed was so urgent, and he so energetic in pursuing it, that there was no room for wasted time or energy. Study was necessary, for background and a basic working vocabulary, but the touchstone in Gold's ideas was, and is, *doing the work.* Why do they call it "the Work"? 'Cause if it were easy, they'd call it "the Play" or "the Relax" (do those sound familiar?)—but it's not.

By 1978, after a stint of California life and another era of personal history I'd need an entire book to describe, I found myself in Tucson again, advertising for a discussion group this time sponsored by me. For this activity, I began to receive the chapters of a book entitled *Work on Self.*

These chapters were by far the best practical material I had ever seen, since each one presented an exercise to be carried out in everyday life, prefaced with a short and forceful description of what aspect of walking sleep and mechanicalness the exercise addressed. Even in that time of burgeoning interest in consciousness expansion and inner work, I never got more than four people to do those exercises with me (I could only draw a dozen or so even for a free seminar or a demonstration of Sacred Dance Movements).

Nevertheless, the format was potent for me personally, and it readily lent itself to an ongoing group practice situation. Each week, we would read the new chapter, go over its meaning carefully, then set our intention to work with the exercise for the coming week. The following week, we would begin the meeting by sharing our experiences and reporting on our results. Often we would decide that the exercise warranted another week of work, and perhaps another. The entire course of "The Big 24," as these exercises came to be known in the circles of individuals who put them into practice, could easily stretch to a year or more, rather than the originally proposed six months.

Before I got through the chapters, they were bound into a private-edition volume, *Work on Self,* and sold as a complete set. By the mid-eighties, after having gone through several printings, this volume which had proved to be an invaluable work-tool had been revised and its vocabulary aligned with the first two books from the author's Labyrinth trilogy: *The Human Biological Machine as a Transformational Apparatus,* a series of essays that brilliantly formulate the introductory theories, and *Life in the Labyrinth,* a *tour de force* on voyaging beyond the limits of ordinary consciousness.

Today, when cultivating transformation and developing consciousness are practically daytime TV material, E.J. Gold has chosen to issue publicly his "Big 24". I for one am enthusiastic that a book this effective will at last be sold on the open market. The question now is, how many seekers are truly ready to stop seeking, to buckle down, look the situation in the teeth, and begin work on the nitty-gritty level of the mechanical, habituated, conditioned primate self?

Regardless of the number of spirit lesson books and soul manuals on the market, there is always room for a "Compleat Idiot's Guide" to the human machine, like that Volkswagen manual we all bought back in the good old days. For that is the difference. *Practical Work on Self* is the lab manual, the portable toolkit for the essential self. But to find that out you'll have to try the experiments, sample the "Big 24", starting from the beginning since the exercises build gently upon one another. Like me, you may come to find this manual indispensable.

These exercises never grow old, never grow stale, and never lose their potency. In fact, they increase intensity over the years, and it should be regarded as a whole-lifetime work.

Work on self has never been easy, certainly isn't warm and fuzzy, sweet and frothy, sparkly and beautiful. It will never be everyone's cup of tea, or a welcome dose of medicine. However, for those who want to work, this is a way I know works, and there is a deep, essential satisfaction in that, apart from all the disturbance, the sweat, the uncertainties involved. The more power to you who can use this book, and I wish for you that, like E.J. Gold's, your efforts may benefit us all.

Iven Lourie
Senior Editor, Gateways

E.J. Gold, *Demi-Monde,* Pastel,
11" x 15", Rives BFK, 1987.

CHAPTER 1

AWAKENING THE MACHINE

The sleeping machine does not—and cannot—produce transformation. A change in Being is obtained only through intense efforts and struggle against our tendency to fall into a state of identification with the machine's sleep.

We must realize that we cannot by mental data and reasoning alone convince ourselves that the biological machine is really asleep, that the Being is identified with the sleep of the machine, and that the sense and aim of human life on Earth—which is to say, the human biological machine functioning as a transformational apparatus for the possible evolution of the Being—cannot possibly proceed in a sleeping machine.

In any case, no one would be able to see the reality of the situation from a mere intellectual argument coming from outside.

We must, in short, deliver an intentional shock; a tangible personal experience in which we see for ourselves that all this is not just some sort of interesting philosophy concocted for our amusement.

We must somehow see, feel and sense for ourselves that the machine is really asleep; we may even see it as actually dead in the grimmest sense of the word.

Until we have definitely seen for ourselves that the machine is asleep, and therefore not conscious in any sense of the word, and furthermore that we cannot make ourselves conscious just by deciding to awaken the machine, we will not really feel the necessity for work.

Once we have felt and sensed the sleep of the machine, even if only momentarily, we know instinctively that we must choose either to sleep away the remainder of our lives or begin to make efforts to awaken the machine.

Four definite forms of consciousness are possible to us:

Horizontal Sleep
Walking Sleep
The Awakened State
Transformation of the Being

Horizontal Sleep and Walking Sleep we can already produce in ourselves without help from a school.

It is the third form of consciousness which we attribute to ourselves but which we ordinarily cannot possess, because it requires the awakening of the biological machine.

We must understand right from the very beginning that this third form of consciousness is not really part of our repertoire, and yet the Awakened State is a form of consciousness which is so basic to life that we ought to be taught as children from our earliest infancy how to awaken the machine so that we can live our whole lives in this state, yet nothing of the kind exists in modern Western educational systems.

The awakening of the machine is to our preparation for a Work life something like kindergarten in relation to university.

If civilization lived up to its name, we would not now be forced to begin our work at such a pathetically low level, but *we must find the courage to realize where we actually stand, and then begin from there*, if we are not to fall into imaginary work.

Our ordinary consciousness resembles a high-steel worker who has fallen asleep while working, yet—just because our work continues and the machine manages somehow to automatically keep its balance—we do not realize that we have fallen into the machine's ambulatory hypnosis.

The machine is conditioned to continue its mental, emotional and physical activities entirely mechanically. Ordinary activities of the machine do not require our attention or presence even to the smallest degree.

When we first come to the Work, we are more animal than spiritual, because we have sacrificed real consciousness for a state in which we are carried along by the routine mechanical activities of the machine as it marches its habitual treadmill to oblivion.

And because the nonphenomenal part of ourselves, through the hypnotic influence of sensation and mental distractions and seductions, falls into identification with the machine's sleep, we will also someday die along with the sleeping machine, never having experienced what it really means to be alive in the machine.

We ordinarily think of ourselves as awake, but if the machine is asleep, we have no real sense of this, and actually it is a lie. The fact is that we fall into identification with the sensory seductions and mental distractions of the machine from the very moment of the birth of the machine to the last moment of its death.

The first intimation of real consciousness is when the machine has been awakened by one means or another and begins to function as a transformational apparatus upon the essential self...what we call the Being. In the course of routine mechanical life, this state seldom happens just accidentally by itself.

We will leave the purpose of awakening the machine until later. It should be enough in the beginning to actually experience the sleep of the machine and to see that this situation can be changed by specific methods which anyone can do with a little practice.

Here is the most surprising little experiment you will ever encounter, by which you can see for yourself the immediate necessity for the awakening of the machine.

Using your ordinary visual apparatus, which is to say, the eyes, follow as intensely as possible the motion of the second hand of a clock or watch or an *Attentiacizer* if you happen to have one, at the same time trying to sense your presence within the machine, including the sounds, smells, temperature, humidity and general ambient atmosphere of the environment; at the same time becoming acutely aware of the constantly changing sensations of the biological machine's skin, the sensations of the internal organs, the sensations resulting from the thoughts passing through the mental apparatus, and the emotions which happen to be proceeding presently within the machine.

All of this while the attention is intensely rooted on the rapid, inexorable motion of the second hand as it moves around the clock-face.

When we first begin our efforts to awaken the machine, the only immediate result is that we soon see that the machine's will to sleep is far more powerful and continuous than our will to awaken the machine. At first the nonphenomenal self can do nothing about this except to exert the only will it really has—the will of attention.

Because we have no will of our own until our will has been intentionally developed, our attention is captivated by the activities and interests which originate within the machine, which is also the source of all negative emotion, all associative mental processes and all negative manifestations.

But we do have the will of attention, and we can actively use this will of attention to observe the human biological machine and its activities both internal and external, without actually trying to interfere directly in the life of the machine.

This subtle activity seems like nothing, but just the fact that we are observing the machine awakens it a little, and our active observation has the effect, although only over a long period of time, of actually altering what is being observed.

At the same time, we can use this exercise to gather the strength necessary to exert a more powerful form of will—the will to awaken the machine...but, as in gymnastics, this type of will takes time to develop.

Because a sleeping machine cannot function as a transformational apparatus, the soul—*which is solely and entirely a product of transformation*—cannot form, and even if it could, without the foundation and "food" for evolution, it could not evolve. If we had the will to awaken the machine, only then could life have any meaning.

Life, as we will come to understand it, is not a progression from the past to the future; it is an Eternal Return, an endless series of passages through, and at right-angles to, the life of the machine, in an effort to perfect it as a transformational apparatus by repeating this passage, eventually repairing it as a whole, higher-dimensional transformational apparatus by awakening the machine from conception to death.

In the course of our Eternal Return through the life of the machine, we must be able to awaken the machine not only in the past, before we ever heard these ideas, but also during its deepest periods of sleep. Only with a fully awakened machine, which is functional as a transformational apparatus from its very first moment of conception, can we perform our Real Work in the higher dimensions.

If we lack the will to keep our source of attention from being seduced into outer world attractions, we will be far too busy with these seductions to be bothered with the task of using our attention to awaken the machine.

This powerful form of seduction which breaks our will of attention is called world-hypnosis, or *Maya*. Maya is often understood to mean that the world is an illusion. We must understand that it is not the world which is an illusion, *but our identification with the phenomenal world,* maintained by The Three Great Enemies—wandering attention, distractions, and seductions.

Nature does not fear ordinary efforts. We must learn to make special efforts, to outsmart Nature, to force Nature to make a mistake, as we would in any game, such as table tennis or chess. Sooner or later Nature will make a mistake—if we do not make one first—and we will be allowed to pass from the influences of the lower dimensions to the influences of the higher dimensions.

We are conditioned to allow ourselves to fall into the sleeping machine and to allow it to continue mechanically in sleep. We quickly learn to become whatever the machine becomes in its mechanical routine.

Identification is not just a simple emotional attachment, a desire to be with someone or something. It is actually the state of falling into the same state as whatever it is that we identify ourselves with, such as the human biological machine. Until now, we have been so completely and continually identified with the mechanical life of the biological machine that we are no longer able to separate ourselves from the machine.

The yogi has learned to transcend the machine, but he is really no better off than any other human being because he has not learned to awaken the machine, allowing it to perform its function as a transformational apparatus upon the Being. He rightly rejects as illusion all the phenomena he sees around him, but cannot see that it is not the phenomena but the seduction of the source of attention into phenomena that is the root-cause of his failure to evolve beyond physical evolution.

Even a sleeping machine can be used to overcome its own sleep *because it has sensations;* we can use these sensations to sense the sleep of the machine. This disarmingly simple idea can be performed as an experiment, in which we try to use the sensations of the machine to sense the sleep of the machine, and from this experiment, we can see for ourselves, in our own experience, several important factors:

- That the machine is really asleep...not just human biological machines in general, but that our machine in particular is asleep, and could even be called "the walking dead".

- That it is possible to see—and even to taste a little—what life can be *when the machine is not asleep.*

- That only by exact and unusual methods is it possible to awaken the machine for any length of time.

- The urgent necessity to begin our work by awakening the machine.

- Why only we are able to awaken our own machines and why no one else can do this work for us.

- That some new unknown source of force for work will be necessary, and that if we hope to continue this work, we will require energies and will on a much larger scale than we are presently accustomed to arousing in the machine and in ourselves.

- That "the Work" is very real indeed and not just an amusing mental philosophy.

- That our time in the machine which we could be using for our possible evolution slips away very quickly and, once lost, cannot be regained.

- That there is a definite deadline for our work, and if we miss this opportunity now, we may not be able to make these efforts later.

These and other realizations will result from the simplest experimental attempt to sense the sleep of the machine.

Once we have tried even for a few moments to awaken the machine by the sheer force of our will, if we can be honest with ourselves, we will never again—until we are able to awaken the machine by the exertion of our will alone—say without squirming at least inwardly, "I am awake".

Trying to awaken the machine for five full minutes by the clock can demonstrate to us the tangible fact of the sleeping machine, the rumor of which comes to us ordinarily only in mythical tales such as *Sleeping Beauty* and *Snow White,* and also at the same time indicates the real possibility of awakening and transformation.

If we believe our machines to be already awake, or that we already possess the will to awaken the machine any time we wish to do so, we cannot prepare for the Work, because we are hypnotized, an utter slave to that imaginary self which speaks of itself in "first person", calls itself "I" without truth, and has a name which gives the illusion of continuity and unity.

Maybe nothing noticeable will happen for a very long time, but eventually, with perseverance, we will obtain definite results.

Not even the Absolute can give us the means to awaken the machine, nor can anyone else activate the awakened machine as a transformational apparatus, thus forming a Bridge between our world and the higher dimensions in which the Being can continue its existence and its work on behalf of the Absolute.

We cannot really call the life of the machine our life; since our will and attention are completely sub-jugated to the will of the sleeping machine, it is the machine's story which we are helplessly compelled to live. When the machine is asleep, we look like monkeys, falling into every external attraction, fas-cinated by all the glitter and flash. When the machine is awake, we cannot possibly act like monkeys, because the presence which is the real source of attention only acts unconsciously *when it is under the influence of the machine in sleep.* We are involuntary victims of the sleeping machine, prisoners to its palpitating self-oblivion, until we are able to exert the will to awaken the machine over the machine's own will to remain asleep.

One method for the awakening of the machine is to intentionally concentrate the fullest possible attention of the source of attention upon the machine's activities. Self-study can now be more closely defined as the study of the motor centrum manifestations of the machine. This is the beginning of all our beginning work.

The mutual-reciprocal transference of the func-tions of the headbrain with the tailbrain, and the resulting awakening of the higher emotional centrum, will be the first active step in our voluntary evolution.

We must understand that before we accomplish this transference of upper brain and lower brain functions we can do exactly nothing—even some-thing as elementary as the invocation of presence

into the present—because the headbrain is incapable of functions beyond the ordinary linear
thought processes which we call "associative-think-
ing".

The headbrain is incapable of real psychology
and does not function for mentation. Its processes
are strictly search-and-follow-a-line, in more or less
spasmodic periodic cycles of active, and more often
passive, reflex-reaction to various stimuli.

If we hope to develop a brain which is capable
of real mentation, attention and will for awakening
the machine and which has all-parts-blended unity,
and a clear uninterrupted vision of the nonphenomenal world, the machine must be turned
rightside-up.

As it is now, the centrums are upside-down. The
thinking centrum is in the headbrain and the
moving centrum is in the tailbrain; the exact reverse
of the true three-brained being called Man.

Human beings of planet Earth are actually two-
brained lower animals into which a primitive third
brain—the tailbrain—was deliberately introduced,
but which functions as a moving centrum, leaving
the headbrain—the real moving centrum—to perform intellectual functions for the machine.

Originally, cross-rhythm exercises were given to
try to force the headbrain to quit operating as a false
mental centrum, but as it turned out, the headbrain
is quite capable of producing cross-rhythms without
too much trouble.

Then, during the *Achaemenid* period of the
Babylonian Empire, mental-psychological exercises
were introduced in large, complicated doses. The

idea was to keep the headbrain so occupied that the ordinary processes of linear associative thought were impossible. But they continued as usual in spite of this artificial mental overload.

Not until the sixth century of the Medieval Period of Western Europe was the idea introduced by schools in the Kurdistan district of what was once called the *Saramoung Province,* that the headbrain could function as a moving centrum, beginning with simple observation, gradually increasing this function by deeper and deeper involvement with intricate movement, following each minute movement of the machine, allowing no detail to escape the headbrain-attention.

After a while, it can be noticed that, if the whole attention of the headbrain is engulfed in the various subtleties of movement of the machine as a whole, parts of the machine, and parts of parts of the machine, the whole process can become a monstrous circus of complexity in which so much attention is demanded that the headbrain is finally forced to automatize its attention on movement, taking responsibility for the movements of the machine, and assuming its role as the true moving centrum of the human organism.

Meanwhile, the poor little tailbrain has nothing to do. Thoughts and ideas begin to pass through it in the same way that fluids pass through a valve, but nothing seems to stick, as it did in the headbrain. Whole vistas of knowledge open, but there is, as yet, no one home to take advantage of all this interesting mental information.

This so-called "unconscious" mind gives us easy access to the whole data-storage system of the machine completely, for the very first time.

When the tailbrain functions as a thinking centrum, the transformational effects of the machine as a whole assist its development into a higher, mental body. Each of the centrums then begins to function as it ought to function.

When the brains are upside-down, the emotional centrum functions as a like-dislike governor, directing the machine and forming habits and moods according to artificial feelings of attraction and repulsion.

These like and dislike habitualities are reinforced in the machine's lower centrums by the inevitable process of psycho-emotional conditioning through repetition over a long period of phenomenal experiences, producing a form of "maze-brightness", such as that which occurs when a rat has learned to automatically traverse a labyrinth.

Then when the centrums are returned to their normal three-brained being functions—that is, the headbrain functioning as a moving centrum while the tailbrain functions as a valve for the flow of thought, the instinctive functions return to normal, and the emotional centrum begins to function for the arousal of exact, voluntary moods and in addition does not interfere in the impartial observation of the machine and its activities.

The newly liberated tailbrain becomes the observing platform for the source of attention which, now that it is free to observe without interference, also provides the all-important force necessary for the invocation of presence.

Transference of the moving centrum from the tailbrain to the headbrain occurs seemingly spontaneously. One night we go to bed unable to mentate or invoke presence, and then, *voila!* The next morning we wake—in the ordinary sense of the word— able to do both very easily.

Of course this change, like all such changes, only seems spontaneous. It happens only after a long period of repeated attempts to force the headbrain to assume the functions of a moving centrum.

To make popcorn, heat and oil are also necessary in addition to the corn itself, to all of which we must add the most important ingredient, *time...* Then, when the corn pops, it only *seems* spontaneous, but if we know the exact causes of this process, we can intentionally repeat this — to the uninitiated — apparently miraculous effect.

There are some for whom this transference has occurred accidentally... If we looked back to what they were doing just before, we would know and understand the cause of their transformation. But they in general have no idea what happened or why it happened. Unfortunately for their associates who follow them around in hopes that something will somehow rub off, one piece of popped corn will not cause other kernels of corn to pop just by association.

There are also in various establishments dotted strategically at several not particularly interesting spots here and there around the planet, inhabitants

of padded cells for whom transference has accidentally occurred.

They have accidentally penetrated the veil
which stands as a barrier between the phenomenal
world and the nonphenomenal world, but without
the necessary preparatory work, unfortunately for
them and to the complete consternation of their
phenomenally fixated medical advisors.

Immediately following the headbrain and
tailbrain transference, one actually may feel even
more enmeshed in the machine than before, in the
mechanicality of it...a maelstrom of automatic conditioning and reflexive motion. Although this sensation seems uncomfortable and one seems worse off
than before, this condition is only temporary.

The very first exercise in a work community is
the observation of the moving activities of the
machine with the ordinary attention of the
headbrain. This observation should be refined to
even the smallest detail, being certain not to alter the
manifestations of the machine as a result of these
observations.

The catalyst-key to this exercise is to remember
while observing that the emotional centrum is not
functional only *because* the brains are upside-down.
When the headbrain acting as a mental centrum
dampens the functioning of the midbrain, the apparatus within which the emotional centrum would
ordinarily arise, no genuine emotions are possible.
The headbrain operating as the thinking centrum
veils the emotional centrum. In electrical terms, the
ordinary human biological machine is completely
miswired.

The wrong connections are made, and the circuit is intermittently-spasmodically dead. When the headbrain operates as the moving centrum then the correct connections to the midbrain are made, and the feeling centrum naturally works by itself, functioning as a higher, voluntary emotional centrum.

Ordinarily, the feeling centrum is impossible to voluntarize in the sense that it can originate its own moods, because as it is, it is forced to accommodate its function to the dominant spasmodic reflexes of the tailbrain.

As the headbrain has very little force, or *will*, the centrum which has the greatest force is the moving centrum. When the mental centrum transfers to the tailbrain, then the mental centrum has the most force and can function in the voluntary.

When the tailbrain becomes the mental centrum, it partakes of the force and authority of the tailbrain, and for the first time has the means to direct the machine as a whole.

Think of the missing keystone cap of the pyramid on the American dollar. This exemplifies the ordinary state of the human biological apparatus. The truncated top of the triangle is the headbrain, acting as the thinking centrum in ordinary man. Adding an upside-down triangle forms the Seal of Solomon. When we accomplish the headbrain-tailbrain transference, as indicated in this diagram of the psychic operation discovered by Solomon—which gave him total authority over those localized fragmentary identities which Solomon decided to call the *djinn,* or lesser demons—all three lower centrums begin to function properly, and more or less in harmony and balance.

But to begin with, we must harness the moving centrum, and force it to become the thinking centrum by removing all its motor-centrum activity by using our will of attention to intensely follow the machine's every motion.

The mental centrum residing in the tailbrain will now have the force and the organic will necessary for real authority over the whole machine. This is the primitive first groanings of real will.

Only then can we be the same tomorrow as we are today, and throw away our cigarettes and really mean it.

The foundation for this work is discipline. If the mental centrum in the tailbrain says, "Wake up, machine," it finally has the will and authority to exert its influence over the machine, and the whole machine is constrained to obey.

Lift the attention from its ordinary fixation on the associative flow of passing thoughts and internal dialogue, and place it strictly upon the moving activities of the machine.

This is an especially good inner exercise when performing physical labor... digging ditches, painting, sanding, building, washing dishes, doing childcare...

For example, say your machine happens at this moment to be using the right arm to lift the cup to drink coffee; observe at the same time how the machine stands on the left leg, right leg slightly lifted; now the machine is smiling, and shifting its weight to the right leg.

In short, use the usual form of attention, but in this case *the subject of attention is now exclusively the posture and movements of the machine observed exclusive of any psycho-emotional significance.*

Ordinarily our movements occur long before we notice them, if we ever do become aware of them, *because we are not trained to fixate our attention on the movements of the machine.*

Most of the machine's activities, the machine performs in secret from us. The machine drinks without our attention; eats without our attention; even makes love without our attention. This is the penalty we pay for allowing the headbrain to operate as the thinking centrum.

After we have maintained our attention on the activities of the machine for a while, its routine becomes apparent, and its activities seem much less overwhelming. After more time has elapsed the once seemingly busy and complex random activity becomes tediously predictable, because in fact, the machine does very little. When we are first beginning to seriously observe, the machine appears to be a maelstrom of chaotic activity.

Watch your hand as if it were a foreign object, but at the same time realize that it is an automatic part of the machine; it fiddles and fidgets by itself without your voluntary direction.

Watch in astonishment as, all by itself, it picks up a fork; note that now the machine is smiling; the hand straightens the knife and smoothes the napkin on the table. And this is only the gross movements of a few parts of the machine, and only on the obvious exterior. When does it perform a wrist-rotation? Which muscles are used?

Different muscular combinations produce varying movements. Not just the hand but everything in the machine is somewhat affected by reverberations. Eventually we should be able to place our attention firmly on all that our machine does. Where is the tension resting when the machine is at rest? Sense the centrum of gravity in the body as it changes.

From time to time notice the centrum of gravity and where the points of weight come to rest. Where is your biggest point of weight? Are you using any force to balance yourself? Suppose you completely relax all your musculature, what happens?

Try to estimate how much force is exerted to keep your body in this posture; do this by sensing.

Tension is measurable only by comparison with relaxation. If we lack the will to relax the machine, we cannot use sensation to determine the exact tension required to maintain a posture. Relaxation and tension must become voluntary for any serious observation of the machine.

Beginning with the observation of the machine's posture as a whole, as if studying a statue—focusing first on the hands, mask, torso, arms and legs, try to see the activities of the machine as a whole unit. For instance, observe your postures sitting at a table, writing in a notebook, walking through a cafe; begin with the most obvious and observable postures and movements. For the moment, until you are very skilled, leave alone those delicate and subtle fluctuations....

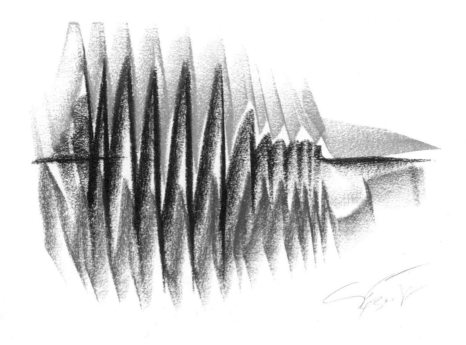

E.J. Gold, *End of Track,* Pastel,
11" x 15", Arches, 1987.

CHAPTER TWO

THE POND

The machine has no real emotion. What we call "emotions" in ourselves are just automatic reflexes of the mental centrum in response to the motor centrum's organic reverberations. Removing the effects of these reverberations eliminates in ourselves the larger part of our negativity and mechanical suffering.

Each human biological machine, according to its own typicality, has its own unique repertoire of reflex mental reactions to shocks, and even to extremely mild stimulations and influences coming from memory, and a corresponding sensitivity to some shocks and not to others.

Shocks are the organic results of impressions passing through the machine, along with the machine's mental centrum responses *to what it thinks it feels* about what it experiences.

As various shocks and impressions impact themselves upon the machine, because we, meaning the nonphenomenal self, have no will over the machine, we are helpless to stop the corresponding organic shocks from radiating outward from each centrum, spreading and reverberating throughout the entire organic system including bone, lymphatic gland system, muscle tissue, organs of ingestion and elimination, blood stream, upper brain, and nervous systems.

Should we be foolish enough to attempt to ingest food, eliminate waste, or reason mentally with ourselves during such organic disturbances, our food will taste terrible, our business and romantic relationships will suffer, and our bowels will refuse to eliminate themselves.

We all suffer from these involuntary reverberations of the machine, especially when the organic machine reacts negatively to these disturbances and takes us along with it.

Think of the biological machine as a calm pool of water and the shock of impressions as a pebble. In this case, the ripples would represent organic reverberations of negative emotions. As we would expect, certain types of pebbles produce greater organic shock than others. When some disturbance makes an impact on the motor-reflexive centrum, it is like a pebble when dropped into the pond; ripples radiate through the machine as a result of the pseudo-emotional impact.

In the example of the pebble dropping through the water, we should be aware that reverberations occur not only on the surface, but under the surface also. While we cannot directly observe these under-water reverberations, we can come to understand that they are very powerful and have a profound influence on our inner states. Of course we wish to keep our nice pond quiet and undisturbed, especial-ly whenever a pebble happens to fall in and disturbs our illusion of calm.

In order to maintain the machine in an awakened state, we must be willing to expend every possible effort to minimize the resulting chaos within the machine whenever it is ravaged by these negative reverberations. We could hide in a cave, hopefully avoiding the pebbles completely. This is the way of the monk, who secludes himself from lower organic influences, hoping that he can remain receptive only to those influences which come from higher dimensions.

But this does not help him in the long run, nor will it help us. In ordinary life we cannot stop these pebbles from falling. We have no authority over these "pebbles", by which is meant external or inter-nal shocks, *nor do we wish to.*

We can have authority over something. But what? If we hope to eliminate these involuntary reflexive organic reverberations in the machine we must take authority over the machine, not in the ordinary way, but *in a very special way.*

We can learn to "open the water" before the pebble so that the biological machine offers no resis-tance to the pebble and reverberations do not occur.

In this way, the negative emotion will at most be only momentary. This exercise is recorded in the Western tradition as *The Parting of the Red Sea*.

Even in the course of ordinary life, we must have occasionally noticed that, when someone who is for us a "walking-source-of-negative-vibration" is near-by, a corresponding sensation begins to manifest itself in the machine, a sensation which we automatically categorize as emotional, and which seems to us very natural. Perhaps the sensation originates in the stomach, maybe a tightening in the chest, or a catch in the throat, ringing in the ears or stinging in the eyes.

After this original sensation, we should be able to sense certain secondary organic sensations which reverberate through the machine, and which only slowly die away after they have thoroughly blended with the totality of vibrations already proceeding in the machine.

Shortly after these secondary reverberations begin to manifest themselves throughout the machine, we ought to notice that the mental centrum has decided that—because the sensations usually associated with one or another emotional state are present in the machine—some emotional state must also be proceeding in the machine.

And this is the totality of what we dare to call in ourselves "emotion". We are unable to distinguish real moods of the emotional centrum from the mental shocks reverberating from ordinary sensations originating in the motor centrum, wrongly identified by the mental centrum as emotions.

If we were able to actively observe the machine over a long period of time, we would notice something peculiar; that the sensations and impressions of the machine change continually in direct relation to these secondary organic reverberations, which we call *negative emotion* because they are produced by the machine.

Mechanical man has no emotion. What he calls "emotion" is really just reflexes of the motor centrum, connected to the muscles and nervous system of the machine. What emotion can there be for a biological machine which functions mechanically according to its conditioned reflexes? Such machines have only lower emotions, imaginary mental centrum emotions in reflex-response to disturbances in the motor centrum.

Because these are not true emotions, but sensations of the motor and reflexive centrums, to which we have learned to attach mental significance, and because they originate in the machine, we call them negative emotions. If they were intentionally produced in the machine's true emotional centrum they would not reverberate throughout the machine and they would be called *emotions,* not *negative emotions.*

Mechanical emotion arising in the mental centrum is only momentary, because it is a reflex of the muscles; it seems to be more lasting only because we see the wake of its destructive passage, its rippling reverberations through the muscles and inner organs.

Real emotions, because they are feelings and not mental responses to muscular reflexes, exist momentarily or continue indefinitely by the decision of the nonphenomenal self. Real emotion is not a personal-subjective mood but a means of emotional communication.

In addition, because real emotions are communicated by the outward radiation of the mood, originating in the awakened emotional centrum, having no reverberational effects in other parts of the machine, it is not necessary to verbally communicate the emotion.

Of course negative emotion, being what it is, which is to say, just a subjective mental state occurring in reflex to a muscular spasm, must be verbalized and elaborately described, explained, rationalized and mentally communicated and understood.

Those who can produce real emotions in themselves never communicate about emotional states in mental centrum language; they just radiate the emotions produced in their machines by the nonphenomenal self, allowing the emotion to speak for itself.

Real emotions strike a corresponding spark of empathy in the receiver. In the presence of someone who is able to produce real emotion, we experience *feelings*—perhaps for the first time. Very often, someone who has awakened the higher Emotional Body and has learned to radiate emotions becomes a celebrity-guru, and people gather like cattle to bathe in the higher emotions. These higher emotions are often mistaken for some mysterious cosmic "force" or interpreted in some pseudo-religious way, but really they are just emotions.

What a pity that human beings are so unaccustomed to emotion that they feel compelled to submissively huddle together in the warmth of the emotional radiation of someone just as mechanical as they are, but who happened to have activated, by accident, the higher Emotional Body!

Negative emotion is useless and destructive. We do not need it for our survival, and, although without negative emotion everyone on Earth would just stand barefoot in the grass and stare blankly at the moon, still, we would be better off without it. Without negative emotion, we can be and do anything, because we are free from our automatic reflexive slavery to the bondage of negativity. Without negative emotion, we can place all our force, will and attention on any aim.

Our reflex reactions toward the manifestations of others are the chief cause of the automatic arising of lower-emotion storms within the machine, if we allow them. When we see someone manifest certain gestures and use a certain tone, we assume that he means by this exactly what we would mean if we used the same gestures and tone.

Negative emotion which arises in this way from our subjective misjudgment about the manifestations of others can easily be eliminated in ourselves. No great effort of will is required for this little alteration in our attitude. Even very ordinary people are able to decide to give others the benefit of the doubt. If we could learn to open the water before these reflexive reactions in the machine, we would no longer suffer the secondary subjective effects in our own machines, resulting from these annoying manifestations of others.

By removing the internal reflexive effects in our own machine—which is to say, the beam in our own eye which responds to the mote in our neighbor's eye—we would eliminate in ourselves the larger part of our negativity and the suffering to our non-phenomenal selves caused by our identification with the human biological machine.

This factor in human behavior is expressed in the ancient saying, "You can't teach an old dog new tricks". Only when struck by some stimulus is the machine able to respond, and then only with just those responses which have by force of habit become ingrained.

For such a machine, the presence of a conscious Being is not necessary for its direction. The biological machine can, just acting under these conditioned reflexes, perform every task and even carry off successfully a serious philosophical discussion at a cocktail party without the participation of a source of attention and consciousness.

Without a special type of will over the machine which comes only with serious efforts over a long period of time, we cannot interfere with the biological machine; it is too powerful to change directly, and we do not know how to slowly influence the machine to bring about real change until we know more about our work.

Trying to change the machine directly is like trying to change the course of a speeding train with our bare hands.

We can use these organic reverberations for our own evolution by containing the outward expression, just as we would contain the steam in a pressure-cooker. This process of containment of negativity can be viewed as a process of controlled alchemical fusion, a method of containing and magnifying the natural chemical and electrical reactions produced by automatic organic reverberations. If we allowed the machine to express these openly, the force for our work would just be dissipated.

But how can we contain our reactions to the annoying manifestations of others? We can see that an ordinary human being is not responsible for his manifestations, that he cannot be. How can we resent or feel anything but pity toward these sad little involuntary spasmodic emotional upheavals, reverberating painfully throughout his machine and leaving a sort of palpitating self-oblivion in their wake?

This condition of complete slavery to the mechanical self should arouse in us some feelings of genuine pity for the state of a mechanical human being. We can use this feeling of pity toward our own evolutionary work, applying the resulting higher emotion of pity toward the activation of the Higher Emotional Body. But if we are to arouse the higher emotion of pity, we must not look down upon mechanical human beings with feelings of arrogance and superiority, because we are all fish from the same barrel, so to speak; no less and no more.

If we can comprehend through our own personal experience that all of what is ordinarily called emotion is really just a secondary reverberation throughout the machine of motor-centrum reflexes, we can begin to take authority over these inner states, because we know the real origin of these emotions, which is to say, the mental centrum's reaction to the muscular system.

We can actually begin to develop the will to awaken the machine just using this special attention in which we deliberately observe the negative states of others, at the same time observing our own machine, remembering that what human beings call *emotions* are just the growlings of the stomach and intestines.

In a way, if we happen to hear about our own machine's manifestations, we are like alcoholics who are astonished to hear about their bizarre drunken behavior, unable to comprehend it because their ordinary state is isolated completely from their alcoholic state.

The ordinary isolation of the source of attention from the machine can give us the feeling that we are not responsible for our own manifestations and emotions and, at the same time, reduce our possibilities for impartial observation of uncustomary emotional states in the machine produced by the unusual emotional conditions which are unique to a work community.

From childhood, we are taught to be acutely aware of the impression we make upon others, and to manifest ourselves whenever possible in a way which would please our audience, in order to win admiration from them.

Our whole preparatory life, if we came from ordinary systems of education, consists in learning how to win admiration or to produce in ourselves by mimicry the manifestations of those who do manage to win admiration. We are educated to continually ignore all our stupid mechanical manifestations, although something must seep through the hypnosis, because everyone in mechanical life spends at least some part of each day worrying whether others have seen him at his worst.

Mechanical man chooses to be aware of only those manifestations which suit his self-love and vanity, rejecting all other manifestations which eventually become for him invisible parts of his outer world. This rejection of certain manifestations and acceptance of others produces a separation, a definite mental-emotional membrane isolating manifestation into two distinct categories, thus creating inner conflict.

The results of this separation of the two categories and the results of containment of those manifestations we reject in the behavior of the machine we will investigate sometime soon. The organic reverberations produced in the machine by the motor centrum reflexes which we call emotions lower the electrical resistance of the biological machine, particularly on the skin. Because negative emotion is produced by the machine and originates in the motor centrum, muscles and nervous system, it produces automatic electrical reverberations throughout the machine.

It is not the original muscular spasm, but the "emotional reverberations" in the muscle and nervous system and the corresponding significance which the mental centrum attaches to these organic reverberations which produce the extraordinary negative effects on our evolutionary alchemical processes proceeding in the machine, destroying temporarily with each emotional storm the machine's function as an apparatus for the transformation of the nonphenomenal self.

Organic reverberation, which depends on electrical force for its continuation, can in this way rise in a spiral to a crescendo of automatically proceeding momentum. It is a force which carries itself in an ever-increasing effect.

Negative emotion, as it reverberates throughout the machine, produces a corresponding alteration in the electrical conductivity of the whole of the machine, and is reflected in changes in the electrical resistance of the skin. When the resistance is lowered, more electrical force is able to pass.

The nonphenomenal self is electrical by nature. All higher bodies are also electrical and produce electrical effects and fields.

If the resistance of the biological machine is too great, and particularly if electrical resistance occurs in parts of the machine, the electrical force of the nonphenomenal self will not be able to flow past this blockage. We can easily see from this that our work to stop the destructive force of negative emotion as it wreaks its destructive force upon the machine—if it is to function as an effective transformational apparatus for our possible evolution—is most urgent for our work.

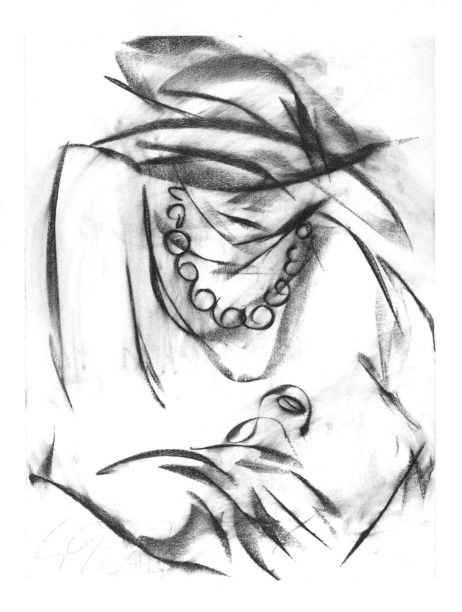

E.J. Gold, *Her Pearls*, Charcoal,
22" x 30", Rives BFK, 1987.

CHAPTER THREE

NEGATIVE MANIFESTATION

Almost everything we say and do is some form of negative emotion, whether we recognize it as such or not. Posture, gesture and facial mask are all inexhaustible sources of negative manifestations.

In general, negative manifestations of the machine are the mental centrum's exaggerated simulation of what it imagines an emotion might be like if it had one, in accordance with the mental centrum's suggestibility to organic spasms occurring in the motor centrum.

When we see an aristocratic lady in a department store, we can, if our attention is sufficiently strong and our own machine is awake, actually see her dreams pass across her facial mask, registered in the facial muscles.

And even if we are not skilled enough to see her dreams, we can at least see that she is asleep and that her attention is distracted, seduced by fascination with all the glitter and flash of the department store, and moreover, that she is completely unaware of her sleep. And in her sleep, unless we do something to disturb her complacent dreams, she will be unaware of our observation.

With experience, we should be able to examine her whole personal history just by observing manifestations and the mask. We notice that she seems to sleep more deeply in what we can see must be her favorite postures and manifestations, those in which she seems most at ease. Occasionally she may become somewhat agitated should the machine awaken slightly, just momentarily, when the machine happens to stop for a moment in some posture she finds displeasing to her vanity, which is itself a mask for personal insecurity.

She does not and cannot know how ugly she is when the machine is in sleep, and if she happened to accidentally discover this, she would be driven into insanity before her personal insecurity became too powerful. At the same time, her machine is so deeply asleep that she is aware only of her own subjective dreams about herself. She has never seen herself as she is, and if she were to happen someday to accidentally catch a glimpse of the awakened machine in a mirror, she would completely fail to recognize the image as her own reflection.

If we were to tell her what we can easily see written on her face, she would be shocked and amazed...but only for a moment or two. Then, in order to protect her vanity, she would find some mystical explanation or dismiss our comments as rubbish.

The personality of the machine, which is to say, its sense of personal identity, is a complex formation of automatically proceeding categorical associations of each of the three lower centrums, the results of organic and psychological conditioning, which became necessary for survival because the machine was asleep from the very beginning.

The real master of the machine, the non-phenomenal self, which is the real source of attention and presence, is very different from the complex personal identity of the machine. It is a simple presence with no particular identity, no particular qualities—although it may take on itself the qualities of its host machine for a short period of time.

Unlike the personal identity of the machine, the real self has no need for embellishment or personal enhancement, because although it is in this world, it is not of it...unless, of course, the machine happens to be asleep and the attention of the non-phenomenal self has become seduced by the machine's dreams.

When we continually express our views and feelings about everything under the sun, as our first-class contemporary civilization teaches us to do, we unconsciously strengthen the vanity and self-love of the machine *for* the machine.

Often we slyly express these mental centrum emotions as indirect forms of negativity, by drop-

ping subtle hints in word, gesture, posture and facial
mask expressions, about our insignificant little personal tragedies of life.

The machine seems to have a virtually inexhaustible repertoire of postures, gestures and facial
masks which can, without actually saying anything,
subtly express negative emotions. These subtle
manifestations of the machine should be closely observed with the ordinary attention, without making
any attempt to use a supernormal attention at this
time. These simple little observations will provide
data for an experiment which will be explained.

The machine, being the mechanical nothingness
that it is, enslaves itself to whatever mood happens
to be suggested by whichever motor centrum posture happens to be proceeding at the moment. These
postures and their emotional reverberations occur in
an exact and predictable sequence according to the
law of the octave, and we can observe them if we
understand this automatic sequence and know
where to look next; which is to say, if we can predict
the flow of tensions, we can follow the sequence
with our attention.

In this way we can begin to exert our own true
will—that is, the will of attention of the nonphenomenal self—over the will of the machine, by
observing the manifestations of the machine, which
has two primary effects:

First, that which is observed is changed slightly
just by the presence of the observer.

Second, the act of observation of the machine
calls for the activation of the source of attention,

automatically activating the higher centrums which eventually form the core of the higher bodies within which we are able to exist in higher dimensions.

Control of the machine's manifestations is not our aim now or later, although the behavior patterns may change somewhat as a result of the influence of the active presence of the nonphenomenal self. And although the effect is slow to assert itself, eventually the attention of the nonphenomenal self upon the machine produces definite changes in the machine, which we will discuss later under the general category of the human biological machine. But behavior of the machine is nothing. The result we are trying to obtain is far beyond the realm of this lower dimension. It is in a much higher dimension that we have our real business.

Every one of us living and working independently toward personal evolution is forced sooner or later to realize that the manifestations of the machine have their origin in an inaccessible monastery which we cannot penetrate in the ordinary way. Yet unless we are able to penetrate this monastery and take command of the machine, we will never develop the will to awaken the machine.

Because the mental centrum is completely inaccessible directly, but can be used as a source of attention for the observation of the motor centrum, and the emotional centrum is completely nonexistent in ordinary human beings, the motor centrum is the most accessible monastery of the inner workings of the machine.

Thoughts and emotions are much faster than movement. Thought passes at the speed of light, and emotion is not much slower. Both are fugitive, changing and passing, as fleeting as vapor. We cannot see them, although we can observe their passage by observing the effects they have had upon the machine, as we would study charged particles in a Wilson Cloud Chamber.

But all this is too complicated for a beginner. Obviously we cannot begin with the observation of pure thoughts and as for emotions—the machine has no emotions in any case, so there is nothing for us to observe!

On the other hand, the motor centrum expresses its manifestations openly and they remain observable for a relatively long period of time; the manifestations of the motor centrum can be observed just by the simple observation of the machine's ordinary activities, using that form of attention ordinarily available to us without special training, which is the attention of the headbrain.

Someday even thoughts and emotions will seem slow in comparison to our accelerated consciousness and deep attention, and at that time, we can work with them directly. But in the meantime, our efforts to use the negative emotions and manifestations of the machine for our own evolution begin actively with the simple observation of all the manifestations of the machine's motor centrum.

We can purify our organic self somewhat by forcing it to fast from food and rid itself of toxic substances. But we can also learn to fast in a very different way, as the pupils in an ancient school once did—from the unwilled appearances of unconscious manifestations, negative emotions originating in the motor centrum.

Make a list categorizing these manifestations of the machine as if you were assembling the data for an encyclopedia of all the motor centrum manifestations of your own particular machine. Keep this list. Eventually you will use it for further exercises. Pay especial attention to that manifestation which seems most precious to the machine's self-esteem, keeping in mind that you are most interested in that particular manifestation under which the machine buries its feelings of personal insecurity.

This manifestation should be studied and imitated until you are able to voluntarily invoke it down upon the machine at your own will, even over the counter-will of the machine.

Practice this particular manifestation many times before the mirror until you are sure that you have it exactly. Then with the eyes closed, do it again, this time *sensing* the sensations of the manifestation, so you can invoke it upon the machine without the mirror.

Using the sensations of the machine to duplicate a manifestation or a posture of the machine is one way to use the sensing apparatus as a tool for evolution. Practicing machine manifestations activates the sensing apparatus which, under the ordinary conditions of life, remains asleep. This exercise produces an intentional bridge across these lower centrums.

Sensing will help us to recognize a manifestation when it occurs spontaneously. So mechanical are these manifestations of the motor centrum that they easily slip past the untrained attention.

When you are able to duplicate the manifestation by sensation, try another exercise: magnify those feelings associated with this particular manifestation so you are able to recognize it with vision, having studied it in the mirror; then by sensing, having studied it with the eyes closed while sensing its "totality", then finally by the feeling associated with the manifestation.

It should be possible for you to practice this manifestation before the mirror or even before a group without feeling too much embarrassment unless you identify with the human biological machine.

Between seeing, sensing and feeling, we should be able to produce a very effective alarm clock which can alert our attention whenever this particular manifestation occurs spontaneously in the machine. To *Keep Oneself* by restraining all expressions of negative emotion manifestations can be work-productive in several ways.

Remember the ancient saying, "Never do anything you wouldn't want to do again." We must not forget as we observe the machine that we are destined to pass this way again, not just once or twice, but eternally. And eventually we will want to wake the machine not just in later life, but throughout its life from conception to death. But what about those periods during which we have allowed the machine to fall into the deep sleep which is visibly represented by its negative mechanicalities?

Of course when we return another time to awaken the machine, even though we may have awakened it before and after these periods of unconsciousness, it will be more difficult to awaken the machine in these negative dramas. We see how difficult it is to awaken the machine under the best of conditions...just imagine what it would be like to awaken the machine during a period of raging mayhem or hysteria!

And what do you suppose it might be like to bring the machine out of the depths of despairing depression?

How would you like to someday spend several thousand passes through your lifetime trying desperately to wear away the rough edges of a period of ecstatic frenzy? What a lot of work we are making for ourselves!

The containment of expressions of negative emotion of the machine means that, before we can really sacrifice anything else, we must sacrifice our own suffering. We often express negativity by casually mentioning problems we have with our outer and inner worlds such as miserable food and not enough of it... Perhaps the weather is all wrong... or we have had miserable sex and not enough of it... We may complain about money, whether too little or too much.

Our biological machine discomforts may be a source of conversation, or our serious world-shaking problems with those who happen not to conform exactly to our standards of behavior and beliefs. We might launch into a nonstop monologue about our pet likes and dislikes. Maybe we hear the machine, to our utter surprise, mention casually the miserable state of public transportation.

Of course everyone is interested in our views about the economy, and our unique situation, which is to say, that we have too many debts to pay and too little pay for the work we do. And what day would be complete without mentioning that our clothing is always the wrong size or we have outgrown it or it is out of fashion just now...?

All these and many more are verbal expressions of negative emotion, negative because it originates with the machine. In fact, everything we say and do, if it originates with the machine, is negative emotion in one disguise or another. And if we are prevented from verbalizing our negativity, we can always find more subtle ways to express our negativity, using little flirtations of the motor centrum.

We must consider how others see and interpret our machine's manifestations if we are to understand how to awaken the machine and use its activities and natural manifestations for our work.

Anyone at all, even someone whose machine is deeply asleep, even horizontal-dead, can see when we feel negative emotion. All our inner world is reflected in our manifestations, like a contemporary poet. We are not able to keep ourselves. We have no authority over our not-overly-domesticated dogs.

To cease to be a helpless slave to our emotional dogs is the very beginning of personal work, and must be mastered before we can take even one step toward voluntary evolution.

Mechanical man is forced to obey these emotional dogs continually, to feed them and play fetch with them when they complain, and yet he believes without hesitation that he has completely domesticated them with himself as their master....

If you really believe this about yourself, just make one little experiment:

Try to stifle all the involuntary negative manifestations of the machine for just one hour and see what happens! If you ever had the idea that these manifestations were voluntary and authentic, you're in for a surprise!

However, we should take heart. It is vital in our beginning work to observe the immense power that the machine holds over the will of the source of our attention, the nonphenomenal self. If we are to win this war, we must understand the enemy.

All those subtle and not-so-subtle manifestations of the machine which express personal urgency, importance, self-esteem, piousness, happiness, embarrassment, fear, personal certainty—anything which might camouflage feelings of insecurity, even something as subtle as casual gossip—should be studied carefully for possible voluntarization.

Each of these categorical manifestations has a definite and recognizable posture, gesture, tone of voice, and facial mask expression, all of which should be studied in detail exactly as one would study a machine or part of a machine.

We will call the repertoire of all these negative manifestations of the machine taken as a whole, *The Crocodile.*

You are to actively study this strange creature from now on, completely, closely, in every little detail, exactly as a scientist would study a newly discovered species.

If you have little love for science and even less for zoology, paleontology, biology or any of the other 'ologies', you could, if you prefer, study the manifestations of the machine in another way, as a role would be studied by an actor preparing a character for the stage.

This should not be too difficult. According to observations, the number of manifestations existing in the human machine repertoire is absurdly limited... so limited that it is almost impossible to distinguish a human being from a store dummy.

As a matter of fact, several times in the course of a shopping expedition, we will find ourselves asking one or another store dummy for the exact time. And conversely we have occasionally been startled to discover that what we had first taken to be a store dummy was a living human being... in the rough sense of the word.

In the course of studying the machine, whichever of the two you decide to use, whether studying the machine as a crocodile or as a theatrical character, try to find that particular manifestation— usually seemingly trivial—upon which the machine depends the most.

It will appear ridiculous to you to even concern yourself with such a trifle, but to others who know you, it is not at all insignificant; just by describing this one little feature you could easily be identified.

This little manifestation, as small and unimportant as it is, nevertheless appears many thousands of times each day and is your most customary posture. Taken as a fulcrum to give us leverage for the observation of the human biological machine, it is called the *Chief Weakness*.

The study of the negative manifestations of the machine helps us to record in our higher mental apparatus all those activities originated by the biological machine, but which we now attribute to our own will and initiation.

Simple observation will bring about slow change through the influence of the non-phenomenal self, using one of the very few techniques which can change our organic habits without making worse ones in their place.

E.J. Gold, *Barlach At Full Tilt*, Pastel,
11" x 15", Rives BFK, 1987.

CHAPTER FOUR

Booby du Jour

Ordinary man is a slave to involuntary restless movements which prove that he has no authority over his biological machine.

In observing the manifestations of our machines, we cannot help noticing that our machines become carried away with various involuntary projects, which is to say, squirm helplessly in their seats.

Although the clarification of these ideas is valuable, the jokes and stories are also part of our work, and can be useful, especially when we know much more and we can see that they not only tell an amusing story in relation to our perception of this world, but that they also refer to events in an entirely different dimension.

A mechanical human being looks like an utterly helpless booby. Why? Because the nonphenomenal self is a slave to the machine, and the machine is a slave to the motor centrum's continual output, resulting in the most bizarre involuntary restless movements. These pathetic spasmodic twitchings are signs to anyone who has eyes to see that we have no authority over our own organic machine.

If we were able to observe impartially these restless manifestations in the workings of our own biological machine, we could perhaps accumulate real nonfantastic data about the inner and outer activities of the machine, and even perhaps someday apply this otherwise wasted negative force for our own work toward the awakening of the machine.

When material is offered which can be used for our observation of the machine, we should learn to use it to observe the machine impartially, without shame. Embarrassment about the machine's activities indicates deep identification with the machine. Impartial observing means we must be prepared to see ourselves as others see us, from outside, not so subjectively.

Eventually we will undoubtedly see many psychological and emotional features about the machine which are not at all pleasing, and may even be horrifying, to our observing selves.

Unconscious actions continually irritate and annoy others, and even if they are too asleep themselves to know exactly the cause of their displeasure, they feel an immediate automatic reflex-of-hatred toward these manifestations.

If we believe even for a moment that our postures and manifestations are self-directed and wholly arbitrary, we are steeped in a self-induced hypnotic illusion.

We could analyze the manifestations of the machine, and if we could analyze them sincerely and impartially, we could see how really limited they are and that our entire repertoire of motor-centrum manifestations consists without exception of habitual postures and involuntary spasmodic semi-faintings from one mechanicality of the machine to another. If we can observe the biological machine as a stranger to ourselves, we should be able to see its activities in an impartial light.

We are never really able to observe the smallest fractions of mental and motor centrum activities of the machine until we have observed for a very long time, and can predict what the machine is likely to do each day. Our observations will become more refined as we come to know the machine more and more intimately. As it is, we have only the most vague general impression of the machine and cannot know, from this general impressionistic view, anything of real value about its life and activities.

In our observation of the biological machine for the purpose of this exercise, we are particularly interested in those manifestations which indicate that the machine is restless, and that our attention has begun to wander, was distracted or seduced, or the machine's will to sleep is greater than our own will to awaken it. We should for the moment confine our observations to these ordinary restless mechanicalities, which we can call our *Booby du Jour*.

Of course we all know that even if we had the strength of ten, we could not possibly contain or discontinue even two or three of the smaller, less forceful mechanicalities; the machine is too subtle and the will of the nonphenomenal self is, as yet, nonexistent. The resulting sensations of frustration, and the remorse engendered by our utter failure to influence the machine even slightly, can serve as the negative force necessary for the awakening of the machine.

Then we can observe the biological machine in its awakened state, and at the same time observe real data about this stranger in which we are carried about all day just like a newborn baby in a self-propelled perambulator.

The effort which we expend in achieving some form of impartiality in the observation of the biological machine is much more important than anything in particular which we happen to observe in the course of events.

In general, each typicality of human machine is completely unique in its repertoire of mechanicalities. One typicality will manifest as do all others of the same typicality.

To really be able to observe the inner workings and organization of the biological machine one must be able to awaken the machine at will, which is to say, by the exertion of the will of the nonphenomenal source of attention over the will of the machine to remain asleep. The observation of the machine then contains the most important factor, *the invoked presence of the source of attention.*

This presence, although subtle and seemingly powerless, is the precise factor which causes the machine to change from a pleasure machine into a transformational apparatus according to the Heisenberg Principle, the law which tells us that the act of observation seriously alters that which is being observed. At the same time, because the machine is awake during observation, the memory function of the higher mental apparatus will retain data obtained during the awakened state for later use in the course of voluntary evolution.

Observations of the inner and outer activities of the machine should not be limited to the period during which we are still excited about it and wish to learn something new. We must learn to take these higher mental apparatus photographs of the biological machine at different times and in different states—not just of small details but of whole actions and in particular of the spasmodic restless movements which we call *fidgeting*. We can use these stupid restless mechanicalities as centrums of gravity for the detailed observation of the activities of the biological machine.

Later on, after a long period of this type of observation, we will observe the machine from an entirely new centrum-of-gravity, which will be the higher emotional apparatus, when we will learn something very different about the life of the machine.

If these mental photographs are sincerely collected by an impartial camera and we have a sufficiently large number of observational samples to study over a long period of time, we are able to view the machine much less subjectively and can obtain a vivid picture of the biological machine—not just from moment to moment but in the longer view, which will help us to understand our work with the machine in the Eternal Return.

Because we are making these observations with the nonphenomenal source of attention and not just the ordinary mental apparatus of the machine, we have established a bridge across the barriers between the higher and lower mental apparatus, and our information will, in this way, survive the momentary life of ordinary memory.

The observation of mechanicalities of the machine organizes our attention and keeps us on guard, watchful for any sign of something unusual which we can use for more advanced exercises of our will and subtle influence over the machine. We must come to understand that the machine is not a real Being, and that we need not feel shame for its activities in sleep but, at the same time, we are responsible for allowing them to continue.

It is our identification with the biological machine which provides the illusion that we ourselves play a part in life and that our part remains unalterable; because as we are in the beginning we are utterly unable to exert our own will over the will of the biological machine; because it is a machine and has an unconscious will of its own, modified by its conditioning.

The biological machine may say and do a thousand stupid things which we never would do if given a choice. We notice helplessly that it becomes restless in one centrum, does something terribly self-destructive, and then to escape the consequences of its actions, shifts quickly to another centrum, then to another... and so it goes.

These stupid, destructive and wasteful little mechanicalities of the motor centrum should indicate to us, as if we needed this additional demonstration, that the machine is definitely sleeping and that it is the motor centrum which is the source of the majority of our manifestations.

After a long period of observation of the biological machine we might become afraid of the machine. We may even come to feel that the machine is our deadliest enemy, just because it spoils our life, systematically and predictably ruining any good impression we might like to make upon ourselves and others.

How can we manifest the beauty of Truth-Absolute when—in the middle of the aesthetic crescendo—the biological machine unaccountably and without our permission, happens to idly pick its nose in public?

We may see ourselves chained to the habits, tastes, sympathies and moods of the machine, with which we have nothing whatever in common. And when the machine runs like clockwork, burying our higher attention in the subtle sleep of routinization, it is even worse, because we cannot see the sleep when everything is quiet on the outside.

We will undoubtedly discover to our horror the real terror of the situation—that our precious force for work is robbed by the continual foot-tapping, scratching and fidgeting—after which, what remains for our own needs? We must somehow learn to stop the machine from flushing this precious energy rightfully belonging to us for our work right down the proverbial toilet.

But, while we may feel gratitude for the biological machine because it brought us to the Work, and we may even feel some mechanical sensations of nostalgia for our earlier innocent identification with the biological machine, which is to say, that mechanical Garden of Eden from which, by partaking of the fruit of knowledge we are ejected, we must not allow ourselves to be carried away by the unconscious yearning for comfort to the degree that we seek refuge—even temporarily—from the evolutionary journey.

In our beginning work, we must be able to accept that, from now on, we will have no place to rest our weary selves, no permanent home, no safe, secure pillow on which to lay our busily chattering heads.

But how, in effect, can we begin to do this? Is there some practical way to "ride herd" on these mechanicalities, the booby manifestations of the machine? We can begin to exert our will upon the biological machine by voluntarizing what has become involuntary and automatic.

Select one habitual mechanicality of the machine which you have observed over a long period of time, making certain that this same mechanicality appears often, at least several dozen times each day.

Now manifest this action intentionally repeatedly over a long period of time, observing the machine. This period serves two primary purposes;

first, to awaken it slightly as it falls under the spotlight of observation, and secondly, to see that it does not change from its usual automatic manifestations.

When manifesting a particularly active "state", if you happen to catch yourself in it—especially if it is very dramatic—suddenly shout *Cut!* and stop the action, like a film director. Then voluntarily begin the action again, loudly shouting, "Lights! Camera! Action!"

Repeat this several times for each dramatic manifestation until it becomes "part of your voluntary". You are now all "movie directors" for the remainder of your personal drama. Now, then... "Lights! Camera! Action!"

Repeat this voluntary performance many times until you can "authorize" its appearance—in the sense of being an author of a story as well as allowing it to occur—and its disappearance. Take the posture of a theatre-director of these voluntary performances with this manifestation; see the machine as an actor playing an artificial role. Take mastery, be firm. Cut to a fine edge the obedience of the actor, then dismiss the character from the stage and use it only when you wish.

Then choose another and follow the same procedure. Master these as you audition them one by one.

This is a student's account of one example of the exercise as it actually occurred in a New York workshop, 1983:

We met as a group in a midtown restaurant which served as one of E.J.'s temporary offices in America. E.J.

had not yet arrived, and as the conversation ranged into the rarefied atmosphere of pure speculation, we all began to be swept away by the momentum.

David had the presence of mind to see the opportunity and shouted, "Cut!" very loudly, so loudly that everyone stopped what they were doing, including the cooks behind the counter.

He rose to his feet, and acting the part of Cecil B. De Mille, clapped his hand peremptorily and commanded, "Let's take that scene again. Places everyone. Lights! Camera! Action!"

To our utter astonishment, the entire restaurant started up again at his command. He repeated this three more times and finally when he felt he could not get away with it any more, he loudly exclaimed, "Print it! That's a take!" and quietly resumed his seat.

We couldn't believe how compliant everyone, ourselves and total strangers included, had been to these commands of his.

E.J. evidently had been sitting around the L-shaped corner during all of this. He clapped his hands and said, "Bravissimo! You had the good sense to stop just before they came to themselves, formed a mob and lynched you!"

E.J. also permitted us to call "cuts" when we caught each other asleep, if the manifestations were sufficiently dramatic; we could call for as many "retakes" as we felt the subject was able to endure.

E.J. Gold, *Maria on the Stove*, Pastel,
10" x 12-1/2", Sennelier, 1972.

CHAPTER FIVE

WORK WISH

We can begin to unify ourselves by creating a special centrum of gravity called our "work wish".

In the ordinary unevolved human biological machine, because its sense of itself is a vague concatenation of all its isolated fragmentary identities, there is no unity which always feels the same about every issue.

Sometimes we feel one way about something, and the very next moment we feel entirely different about it. Our lack of unity produces in us a corresponding lack of will. In mechanical man nothing provides a permanent centrum of gravity for unity. We can make the beginning of unity by creating in ourselves a special temporary centrum of gravity which we can call our *work-wish*.

A work-wish is an artificial aim which has become—of course only temporarily—more important than anything else in life, at least until it has satisfied our purpose, which is the early development of unity and will. For the purpose of this experiment it is necessary that we learn to do everything only in relation to this special artificial work-wish.

If we were to continue life in the ordinary way, all our conflicting inner impulses would eventually neutralize each other into apathy or some vague monomaniacal compulsion, until finally, under the dreadful spell of senile psychosis, we would drift helplessly and aimlessly toward the quick brown fox of ordinary death like lazy dogs.

We survive only so long as we have the ability-to-wish. The continued survival of our wishing has the unique property of allowing us to complete our work, but for this aim to have any real effect, whatever wish we have formulated must be greater than, and have real existence beyond, our own short and insignificant lives.

Ordinary desires are much smaller than ourselves, so we must discover something which is greater. Unfortunately, the majority of our understanding is limited to what is smaller than ourselves.

If we could see the personality of the machine dissected into its primary component parts, we would see a complex inner disorganization of many fragmentary identities, each with its own power, thoughts, feelings, beliefs and, in particular, its own manifestations.

Each of these fragmentary identities is convinced that it is able to act independently and has complete authority over the biological machine, and they are all convinced of their unique right to call themselves "I" when referring to the overall identity of the human biological machine. In this complex disorganization of parts, unity can only come as a result of a serious effort over a long period of time to blend its parts into one balanced whole.

In mechanical life such blending can never happen just by accident. Only by intentional inner alchemy can we force such a blending of these isolated fragments of the machine to occur, which in turn produces a machine able to function in the Work. Without unity, the machine would soon wander into distractions, making our continued work in the Work unreliable and eventually impossible.

To begin the inner alchemical process we must start with an imaginary aim which we hope, by repetition over a long period of time, will someday become real. This can bring no result if we try it just once or twice; we must understand exactly what it is that we are trying to do.

Knowledge and understanding, data and experience, each hand washes the other.

Only with a clear idea of our aim can a change be made by imaginary beginning efforts. An imaginary effort can become a real effort only drop by drop, as in any distillation process.

Before this experiment, and before any experiment from now on, we should always remember to wish that our efforts be for the benefit of all Beings everywhere, to make a wish of greater force than just wishing for ourselves.

The effectiveness of our wish depends on whether we are able to collect the *force of necessity.* This "wishing-for-all" made inside ourselves can connect us someday with the Mystical Body of Christ which always exists outside time itself through all ages, including long before the man called Jesus lived and died.

The Sly Man may or may not have this or that attainment, but one thing is certain: by himself *because he has attained impartiality even toward his own aims,* he has no necessity of his own. Yet at the same time he may have a soul which suffers unutterably each additional day he is forced to spend in exile.

The Sly Man is forced to become a teacher; he is also a thief, forced by destiny to help himself by helping others, but to whom can he turn? Everyone of his own gradation is in the same boat. He must seek help elsewhere through his own efforts and labors.

He can find many who have necessity but who have not the means or the doctrine. He can find a way to entangle them in his sphere of influence so as to force destiny to provide a means for his pupils and at the same time provide him with the necessary understanding to continue his work. He must already possess knowledge.

If his pupils can be made to have genuine necessity and not just curiosity, and at the same time be cut off from all ordinary sources of help, the Sly Man can, while transmitting the means for satisfying the needs of his pupils, also take for himself what he needs. In this way he can make a necessity for himself without having a genuine self-necessity.

The Sly Man is forced to become an expert in providing for others a genuine work-wish, particularly toward just that aim for which he is working at the moment.

Mechanical man has no necessity by himself, and no means to discover the Doctrine for himself. He cannot make a Method for himself, and is in this way dependent on the Sly Man for his initiation into the Work and for his beginning efforts.

The Sly Man has learned that only by wishing for something greater than himself can anything of value be attained for himself. He can learn and take what he needs by providing for his pupils what they need for themselves. Of course he must also provide them with the need which they are then compelled to satisfy.

By laboring for others we can intentionally receive for ourselves what we need. To make a wish greater than ourselves we must learn to conform to the laws of work-necessity. We can learn these laws and apply them as needed, as long as we consider and respect those others who are drawn into our work.

We must learn to put others before ourselves, serve their needs before our own in order to fully take advantage of this technique by forming study circles and giving them what we learn.

A work-wish can be a deliberate wish against the slave impulses of the machine. With no work-wish as a centrum of gravity we never develop the ability to exert our work-will against the natural slave impulses of the biological machine, the wishes of centers and parts of centers to remain asleep. The machine has within itself many small sources of influence, both internal and external and, without work wishing, these need not be very strong to have the machine—and the nonphenomenal self along with it—under their power.

But the human being who is all machine believes himself to be very powerful, to have free will and the ability to do anything he decides to do, except take out the garbage, flush the toilet and remember to mail a letter. He is so powerful that he is only a slave to sex, drugs, alcohol, tobacco, coffee, candy, sports and a vague sense of political issues.

We must have an exact purpose. When we can understand an exact purpose for ourselves, we will be able to compose a corresponding work-wish and only then receive some beginning help toward that specific aim. No one can help us to attain some vague purpose, nor can anyone tell us what wish to make for ourselves. Each one must ponder and consider his or her purpose in the work circle.

Ultimately we must learn to make a work-wish from everything we do in life, to make all our activities work-significant and give them force by wishing that the results of all our efforts be used for the greater good of all beings everywhere.

Now I will give you a small work-wish you can use for your self. When making the sacrifice of anything for your work, such as one lower emotion, one cigarette, or one drink of "booze", say with the fullest possible force of your inner self, *"I wish the results of this small sacrifice to be used for the benefit of all Beings everywhere,"* and make this wish reverberate in your solar plexus.

This special wishing can be used for anything to which we are a slave and know we are a slave, even for the "palpitating-loss-of-self-during-involuntary-orgasm."

We must examine our wishing to see impartially if it is greater than our self. We must work not with the hope for something which is not, but with that which we already have. To wish is not a synonym for hope or for desire.

You wish for a higher existence without even pondering for a moment what it might mean to be a higher Being, what the responsibilities and obligations might be that go along with it.

Everything has a price, but you never ask how much you must someday pay and in what currency, and no one else can pay for your work.

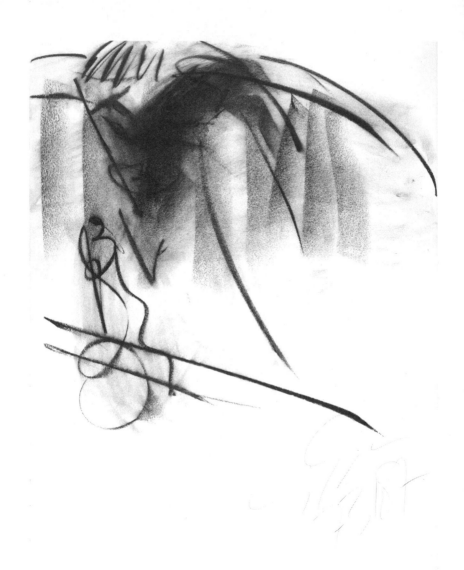

E.J. Gold, *Dominance & Submission,*
Charcoal, 22" x 30", Rives BFK, 1987.

CHAPTER SIX

STRUGGLE OF THE SORCERERS

Ordinarily the war of the forces of darkness and of light just happens mechanically within the machine. It is uncontrolled and wasted. We must find a way to organize it and make it profitable to our work.

The Teacher may set the stage and throw the spotlights on something of importance, but ultimately you are the directors, stage managers, choreographers, dancers and audience of your work-ballet.

A ballet of work can be staged if only we know the characteristics of its two powerful mutual antagonists: The Prince of Darkness, who dwells in darkness and whose vision is fixated on the light representing the awakened forces of light, and the

Prince of Light, representing the sleeping forces of darkness.

Although they both use the same methods and their armies are composed of exactly the same soldiers, when one or another becomes active, their minions are of two completely opposed characters.

The attention of the followers of the Prince of Light is fixated on the objects of fascination which are common to the sleeping state of the machine, and is violently opposed to the awakening influence of the followers of the Prince of Darkness.

Ordinarily their warfare is not organized and therefore is useless for our work. We must find a way to organize their war and make it profitable to our work, in much the same way that munitions manufacturers and other industrialists foment and feed a war, by providing materiel and continually aggravating the antagonists against each other. It is in our interest to keep them in continual struggle.

In the ordinary human biological machine we find—if we take the trouble to look—deep contradictions of feelings, thoughts, memories, phrases and manifestations, all of which are isolated from one another by memory buffers, each only one small fraction of some unknown and chaotic whole.

All these are quite powerfully opposed to one another and if they were not isolated by powerful mental and emotional buffers, they could not exist peacefully together in the same organism.

Science will one day come to discover that every single cell in the muscular system of the machine can function as a storage sector for moods, ideas, manifestations and memories. These are stored at random, without regard to logic or reason because there is no presence of attention which is able to correctly categorize each impression as it enters the biological machine. If we were to suddenly see and not just vaguely feel all these contradictions in ourselves at the same time, without the usual organic buffers, we would feel that we had gone mad.

In order to function, the machine has, somewhere along the line, placed buffers as isolating devices between these inner contradictions. It is because of these buffers that we are ordinarily able to exist very calmly despite our continually shifting centrum of gravity and a different set of opinions, ideas and moods every moment or two.

A human machine cannot live long without buffers; either the contradictions must be isolated in some way or the machine must be tucked safely away in the lunatic asylum.

While the machine cannot exactly destroy its conscience in order to be free to seek perpetual gratification, the emotional centrum, which is the activating factor of conscience, can be put to sleep by isolating the machine's contradictory states. These contradictions, if taken all together, form the fragmented identity of the machine.

It is thanks to the incessant chatter of automatic inner dialogue and running commentary on our experience which goes on continuously between these isolated fragmentary identities, that we attribute to ourselves what we call consciousness; in a rough translation of Descartes, *I talk to myself, therefore I am.*

All this cannot help affecting adversely the transformational function of the machine; these very strong buffers have arisen in the machine over the course of years in order to prevent total breakdown. Should these buffers be tampered with by an amateur, such as the contemporary clinical psychologist, the biological machine is quickly reduced to the unquestioning compulsive madness of ordinary social-organic pursuits.

It is vital to understand that this artificial isolation occurs only because each facet of personality is stored in a different part of the machine. This occurs haphazardly and any part of the machine's personality may be stored anywhere and be activated into reflex-response by the most seemingly unrelated stimuli.

In the study of these buffered contradictions, we must notate and categorize to ourselves the various states of our fragmentary identities which we are able to observe as they become active in the machine. It is to these fragmentary states and not to ourselves that we should attribute all our attitudes, ideas, power, initiative, presence and good taste.

The human biological machine is directed by the machine's simulation of intelligence, not the real intelligence which could be provided by the presence of the nonphenomenal self in the awakened machine.

In a human biological machine in which each buffer encapsulates a fragmentary identity, a continually shifting centrum of gravity changing in what may appear to be random patterns provides the appearance of a very complicated gem of many facets, but which is actually a very uncomplicated lump of carbon in the grip of certain laws from which we can free ourselves by awakening the machine.

The machine's story is a revelation of these contradictions, and by a true confession we can effect their eventual reconciliation, which we can call the *Process of Redemption.*

By telling the real life history of the machine and not some fragmentary fantasy composed for the protection of the vanity of the machine, thus blending these contradictions, we can repair the past and redeem the machine as a transformational apparatus.

To blend these contradictions it is only necessary to remove the buffers which have been placed between them, which is accomplished by the gentle art of exposure to the light of confession.

Ordinarily we know only one third of the life story of the machine at any given moment, depending upon which fragmentary identity is active at the time. In this sense, that side of ourselves which we believe we know best and which seems to us to be our only friend is actually our deadliest enemy in the Work.

In addition to telling the true story of the machine's life, we can use daily situations with potentially conflicting aims to help us stage the ballet *The Struggle of the Sorcerers.* For example, when we are tired we can refuse to lie down and rest; we may even do very hard work like dig a hole or build a wall. We can, if we are attracted to sweets, place before the machine a mound of chocolate and then for as long as possible—at least as long as it takes for

the candy to rot—deny ourselves this little indul-
gence. Of course, after the candy rots away, self-
denial is easy.

We can force our biological machines to work at
a different tempo than usual; we can refuse to express pleasure or displeasure in the usual ways; we
can intentionally keep company with someone who
ordinarily repels us, especially one whose chemistry
repels us.

To force conflicting ideas to reconcile we must
be able to, if necessary, lie down and at the same time
convince ourselves that we are standing. These
small conflicts are easy to arrange. Later, to stage a
real ballet, we must entangle these two powerful
sorcerors in a genuine struggle for survival. The
ballet must have a great conflict in order to attract
and hold a struggle between these great forces.

No matter which side wins, it comes to the same
end, because both roles are played by the same
actor—the empty struggling against the void.

E.J. Gold, *Circle of Friends*, Pastel,
10" x 12-1/2", Sennelier, 1987.

CHAPTER SEVEN

THE SEARCH FOR DR. LIVINGSTONE

When we have no real identity we can become anything suggested to us by inner and outer influences; we believe ourselves to be whatever we fall into.

Just now at this moment, we may think of ourselves as nothing more than a stupid mechanical apparatus for the transformation of organic material of one kind into another form of matter more suitable for the fertilization of flowers.

Yet, just yesterday we thought we were Mr. God Himself!

When our identity is immersed in the machine's sleep, we think of ourselves as the machine and we are subject to the subtle and not-so-subtle suggestions of inner and outer influences upon the machine.

During the course of the day—if we happen to remember to observe the activities of the machine— we may come to notice the inevitable passages of the machine through one mental identity after another. If we observe the machine over a long period of time, we can actually see these continually changing roles. Through careful observation of the machine we can see clearly that as long as we are identified with the sleeping machine, we are not the same today that we believed ourselves to be yesterday. Yet the myth which we most believe about ourselves is that we are the same.

We believe ourselves to feel the same and think in more or less the same way from day to day and even from year to year, yet we have ample proof that this is not so.

We live in an age of reason, of high moral aims, yet this century with its Hitler and Mussolini, its crimes in the name of Christ, is no different than the butcherous days of the Medieval period when soldiers marched from Western Europe into the Holy Land to commit legendary atrocities, which were repeated during the Inquisition and were really no different from those atrocities committed by Attila the Hun and the delightful Roman Emperor, Caligula.

And these people did not act alone; they had ample help from "reasonable" people, who thought of themselves in much the same way as we all think of ourselves, as basically good people who only want peace and quiet in our lives, who want to be left alone to enjoy the pleasures which life has to offer.

The point is that we see ourselves in one light, and yet underneath it all, we are savages. The machine cannot be trusted to be the same today as it was tomorrow, nor can we hold ourselves really above the machine. We have so little will that regardless of our mental decisions and our highest aims, we are unable to change anything in the machine. Because it is constantly changing, and because we are identified with the machine, we change with it.

The machine carries us helplessly along on its merry path to self-destruction. Do you think for a moment that things are any different inside the machine than they are outside it? History is a reflection of our inner natures, and our own internal conflicts very much resemble those of the outer world. We each have our inner Hitler, our own unique Caligula, our barbarians and ranting maniacs.

But we do not think of ourselves in this way, because our blithely philosophical mental centrums, tucked safely away in their ivory towers, are not in direct contact with these deeper, more animalistic parts of the machine.

The fact is that we can make any aim for ourselves quite easily with the mental centrum, but when it comes right down to it, we haven't the will to drive our aim down where it counts, right into the flesh and blood of the sleeping machine. Where then are we to obtain the will necessary for the awakening of the machine and its subsequent use as a transformational apparatus?

We must now consider the very distinct difference between our real identity and the identity of the machine. To begin with, the real self, the nonphenomenal self, has no will of its own beyond a will of attention, which is to say, it is only capable in the beginning, until it has developed a greater will, of simple attention. Even this, if we know how to use it, is a powerful weapon against sleep. In order to use this will of attention, we must first definitely establish our own true identity as distinguished from that of the machine.

The real identity never changes. Imaginary identities continually change. We believe ourselves to be whatever we fall into, just like children at play who eventually come to believe in their fantasy.

Only when we have established an identity which is free from the sleep of the machine have we established the true source of attention, which can then actively and impartially observe all the activities and manifestations of the machine from the platform of this new and unchanging self. This station for the impartial observation of the machine is often referred to as the "third eye".

If we happen to observe a temporary machine-identity while it is still active, we can remember to identify with the nonphenomenal source of attention by rejecting identification with the machine's state, saying to ourselves "I am not this". But this effect is only obtained *while the momentary machine identity is still active.*

All ordinary identities originating from the machine are eventually replaced by other identities which, because they are changeable, are obviously not the authentic self. When we are identified with the sleep of the machine, our attention is, by association, under the continual influence of the distractions and attractions of organic life.

Every moment we work to awaken the machine can be an opportunity to regain our real identity.

Identification with the changing self produced by states of the machine distorts our understanding of the Real World. When we are able to draw back momentarily from the sleep of the machine, we can see that we have fallen into a machine-originated identity. If we are able to exert the will to awaken the machine, we can see that we have fallen into the sleep of the machine and can say to ourselves "I am not that".

Having fallen into a machine-identity, we can learn to separate ourselves from it by remembering, "I am not that," "I am not that," rejecting all those identities which are *not* eternal and unchanging, trying to discover in ourselves that one true identity which does not and cannot change.

We can use this method of rejecting false identities to discover the true unchanging self in more or less the same way that Stanley tried to find Dr. Livingstone in Africa.

Combine this search with your other exercises, using the machine's impermanent and transient identities to remember to identify not with the sleeping machine which is the source of these fragmentary identities and states, but with your nonphenomenal source of attention, until you find your own "Dr. Livingstone".

E.J. Gold, *Macro Personnage Limbs Akimbo,*
Pastel, 11" x 15", Rives BFK, 1987.

CHAPTER EIGHT

HARMLESS WHIM

To gratify a harmless whim can be a beginning method of accumulating the will to awaken the machine.

Although we can never really stop an automatic manifestation of the machine until we are able to exert the will to awaken the machine, the effort—although guaranteed to fail—can serve as a reminding factor to activate the attention and, at the same time, we can use the inevitable feelings of frustration to help us to awaken the machine.

In the struggle against the machine's automatically arising negative manifestations, we are helpless alone, but we can form a work-circle, a circle of friends, who can try to help each other to remember to struggle.

Any human being, with a minimum of effort, can learn to live in the higher dimensions. With the freedom we now have to teach these ideas, although this will change very soon, nobody really is forced to remain buried in a sleeping machine.

The very beginning of this new life in which we prepare ourselves for life in the higher dimensions begins with the solemn vow to never again allow the machine to manifest negativity.

Those who knew us before may consider us less interesting than we were before, because our machines no longer manifest so easily, but this is the price we pay.

When exerting an effort to invoke our presence and to contain negative emotions and manifestations of the machine, why should we worry about the impression we make on others? After all, they will all be dead soon anyway, if they aren't already.

When we make efforts to take responsibility for the manifestations of the machine, we also gain the will to awaken the machine and, at the same time, activate the higher centrums to some degree. But the nonphenomenal self has no will other than the will of attention.

We can influence the machine in subtle ways, as a woman exerts her influence over a man, but we cannot act directly upon the machine. Because we have no will over the machine, we cannot oppose it. On the other hand, we can use the force of the machine's own power to overcome it.

Deliberate exaggeration of a negative manifestation can help us to gain will over the machine, eventually bringing the manifestation into the voluntary. When it is voluntary, we are able to manifest it or not, as we choose. Involuntary habits cannot be activated intentionally, or stopped at will. A first step in the attainment of will is to voluntarize every habit.

To gratify a *harmless* whim can be a method of activating Real Will, which is to say, the will of the nonphenomenal self to awaken the machine over the will of the machine to remain asleep.

We must take especial care not to cultivate these whims into something bigger than ourselves, so much so that we become enslaved to them as we are to our ordinary desires. Small things we do not really want for ourselves are the only things we can really call "whim".

To compel the machine to do one small thing not desired by our organism or personality and also not automatic in the conditioning of the organism gives us a taste of Real Will on a small scale.

The Transformed Being stands on the edge of Creation, facing the unknown, the not-yet-manifested. The sleeping machine is enslaved by the past and can only re-enact what has been. The future is the past. Time is the key, but to open this door, to penetrate into the present, we must develop the will to awaken the machine.

The machine has no real will. What it calls "will" is just strong desire. A machine with powerful desires is said to have real will, and a machine with weak desires is styled a "weak person". If we sacrificed everything in life just to gratify one or two powerful desires, we would be said to be a person of strong will. But even a very powerful dog will some-day die like a dog.

Because everything in the machine is isolated and fragmented, its state can change radically in one moment. It can explode in the throes of a personal disaster which seems to be the end of the world just by one small change in diet, sex, or even as a result of an unexpected change in the weather.

Often what we call free will is simply accom-modation between conflicting desires and repul-sions. The usual result of this artificial mechanical will is either hesitation or blind certainty.

We think of these mechanical impulses as manifestations of our "free will", just because we seem to be able to choose, of course guided by our conditioning, between hesitation and stupidity.

But the machine is just a machine and the machine will always make its decision whether we are aware of this or not.

Choose for yourself several small whims not presently existing in your ideas of self-gratification, but be sure these are not important. It is best to choose impartially, or at least suspiciously, so that you do not choose something which the organism or personality would like.

Find something *you* would like to gratify for your self. If it is mildly disturbing to the organism or personality, so much the better, but be certain it is not disrupting or dangerous.

Then deliberately gratify these whims. So long as everything remains harmless, to yourself and most of all to others, go to the most elaborate lengths possible to gratify them. The smaller and more insignificant the whim, the better, but again I caution you...always maintain harmlessness to yourself and to others.

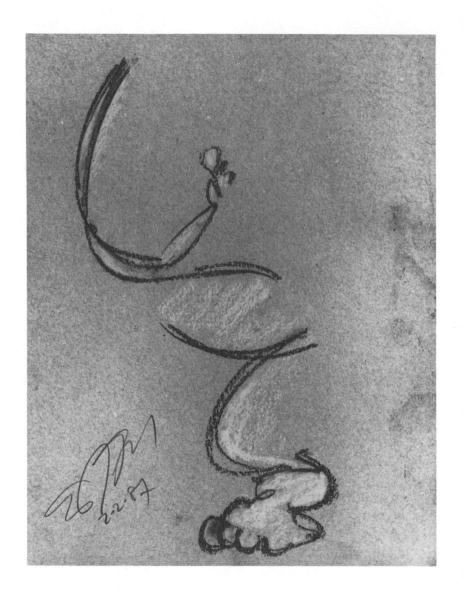

E.J. Gold, *Mirror Reflection*, Pastel,
10" x 12", Sennelier, 1987.

CHAPTER NINE

ONE SMALL HABIT

As we struggle with the machine, beginning with one small habit, we can produce an "alchemical fire" in the machine's chemical factory, which will gradually transform our Being.

The functions of the mental, emotional and motor centrums operate independently but in "reciprocal passivity", changes in one inevitably affecting the others. When one changes its activity the other centrums correspondingly compensate for this change.

Any intentional change in the motor centrum will produce a corresponding change in the moods and thoughts of the mental centrum.

Even though as nonphenomenal Beings we have no direct will over the machine, at least in the beginning, we can enlist the aid of the mental centrum in the tailbrain; a small exact change can produce corresponding changes in the ordinarily inaccessible "monasteries" of the reflexive, feeling and thinking centrums.

After a while, with repeated efforts, we can gain sufficient leverage in the machine to activate the higher centrums. In ordinary life, we never change our comfortable habitual postures and movements, and so nothing can happen outside the ordinary routine of the machine.

Even if we wished intensely to change the habits of the human biological machine, long impartial observation is necessary to be able to categorize the habits which are presently operating in the machine.

Habits are so completely automatic that our nonphenomenal attention is blind to them. We are not able to study the habits of the machine directly, because when we exert our attention upon the machine, the machine wakes up a little and the habits disappear momentarily.

The most difficult manifestations to observe are those tiny little unconscious habitual expressions of the motor centrum. The smaller they are, the harder they fall. To be able to gather data about the very smallest negative manifestations, those most automatic, we must receive help from outside because the machine cannot be trusted to give us correct information about itself.

A work-circle is useful for this, because in the beginning we really cannot see the manifestations of our own machines with enough impartiality to categorize them.

The habits of the motor centrum are so trivial that we may not be able to see them without special help, and for this we must use a group of people engaged in similar work, who can see our machines with much more objectivity than we can ourselves. Naturally, they may miss one or two particularly revolting manifestations, but leave that for later. Sometimes an outside observer can catch us in an uncustomary posture and delineate it clearly to us, even considering our clouded vision.

The whole life of the machine from beginning to end is a pathetic little habitual dance, something that just happens to us while we are busy making other plans.

But if we begin a struggle to observe the habits of the machine, even if at first we are blind to them, starting with smaller ones and gradually overcoming bigger ones as the strength of our own attention increases and dominates the attention of the machine, we can produce in ourselves an "alchemical fire" which gradually can transform the inner self of the machine into an activated transformational apparatus. We must somehow learn how to keep this fire burning.

We can begin this process by concentrating on one small habit of posture, gesture, tone, mood, work, waking, sleeping, eating, tying shoes... something small, some little unconscious habit which occurs several hundred times each day and which can serve as a little alarm clock—a reminding factor—for our beginning work to awaken the machine.

For instance, I know a person whose machine
has a little habit of saying "is it *ever!*", a habit of which
the source of attention within that machine is completely unaware. And her source of attention is unaware of this little habit precisely *because it is a
complete mechanicality,* an unconscious habit which is
so small, so insignificant, so automatic that it has
become a seemingly natural part of the machine's
repertoire. Yet anyone else can see and hear this little
habit, and recognize immediately that it is out of
place. To others it is a shock because to their machine
it is not a part of their own automatic repertoire.
When her machine announces "is it *ever!*", she does
not hear it, but others immediately see it as something unusual.

It is this invisibility of our own machine's habits
which makes group work necessary. While we cannot see our own mechanicalities because they form
a part of our view of the general "rightness" of the
universe, to others our habits are definitely out of
place, and therefore visible. In a group, we can help
each other by suggesting little habits which can be
used as what we could call "cattle prods", electric
wands used to direct cattle.

The objective observation of small habits of the
machine which are invisible to our own vision is one
useful function of a group and, in spite of all the
discomforting factors inherent in working with a
group, is one of those things we just cannot trust
ourselves to see objectively enough to actually use.

We should have no trouble whatever gleefully
pointing them out in each other because our

machines will undoubtedly find the unconscious habits of other machines extremely annoying.

We might wish because of our vanity and self-love to eliminate these bad habits which we discover in this exercise, and to substitute good ones, by which we mean "manifestations pleasing to everybody else, and most of all to ourselves," but we must understand that a habit cannot be eliminated without substituting another one in its place; nature abhors a vacuum and inevitably fills it with something similar to what was there in the first place.

Something unwanted and possibly even worse may take its place, something which may make us unable to remain in a work-community.

Our new habits will be no better than the old, *because they are conceived in sleep,* and may even allow the machine to fall more deeply asleep than it was before.

How fortunate we are to have a sleeping machine, full of negative force and thousands of little unconscious mechanical habits!

Whenever we happen to overhear the machine saying or performing something from this almost unlimited storehouse of mechanicalities, we can use the inevitable electrical shock—however small the voltage and current—as a cattle prod, providing us with just the amount of electrical force necessary to awaken the machine!

Now we have enough data to generate a list of all those annoying little repetitive mechanicalities of the machine which could serve as "cattle prods".

E.J. Gold, *Enwrappedtured,* Pastel,
9-3/4" x 12-1/2", Sennelier, 1987.

CHAPTER TEN

MENTATION

Mentation is the force of collected attention which activates the Higher Mental Body.

We use the term "mentation" to mean the intentional processing of ideas in the mental apparatus in more or less the same way that a blacksmith would handle iron.

In this sense, mathematics and motor centrum exercises in which various parts of the body are moved in opposing rhythms are good discipline for preparing the mental apparatus to handle the controlled mental flow of thoughts to an exact end result.

In mentation we use a special form of will to keep the mental apparatus on a specific path.

Meditation is a polite euphemism for a mild form of pondering. To produce real mentation from out of our wandering thoughts, which are ordinarily guided by the flow of automatic association, we must add another ingredient, something unknown to ordinary human beings, and which they have no data in themselves to be able to discover by any ordinary means.

Mentation can be said to be the artistic and proficient use of the lower mental apparatus which elevates it from a strictly mechanical organ in which thoughts are processed by the flow of automatic association in which one thing suggests another and one thought drives out the previous one, to a real centrum in which attention of presence can become active.

The machine cannot imagine thought which occurs independently of the process of automatic mental associations.

If we should happen to accidentally somehow hear about this idea of mentation before we come to a school, we inevitably decide that it must mean the deep passive observation of the automatic flow of whatever vague thoughts happen to be proceeding in the mental apparatus at the moment.

In ordinary thought, we do not care what may happen and cannot direct our thoughts except in the most general way, and after only a few minutes at most the attention wanders, becomes distracted or seduced, and we forget our original aim entirely.

For mentation, we collect all those ideas which happen to fall within the same general category and focus upon them unremittingly, fixating them in the high-intensity spotlight of a special form of will of the mental centrum, called *concentrated attention*.

We can turn back and pick up all the attention we have scattered behind us all over Creation in much the same way that a child leaves a trail of clothes behind him when he toddles off to bed. This little, but powerful, ingredient of "collected attention" is to mentation what the fulcrum was to Archimedes.

Then, taking any object, such as this ashtray, we can concentrate our full attention on it until no interruptions from other sources of interest occur. Have a *seance* with it, looking, listening, feeling it... We establish a new organization of the nervous system as a result of this new mental activity.

Now try this same concentration of attention on an organic part of the machine, then on a thought, then on trying to recapture a mood from your childhood by intentionally reproducing its sensation in the present.

Mentation is not an end-in-itself, and we are not interested in control or personal manipulation of the machine.

Let us pause for a moment to consider...what is the use of mentation? If we do not know the use of mentation, what can we possibly learn from it? After all, we do not wish to become just passive mental philosophers.

We must have heard the idea that by this discipline of mentation, because the headbrain functions strictly by association and cannot mentate, the machine eventually learns to activate the higher mental centrum.

In Atlantis there existed a great crystal and many smaller crystals taken from the larger crystal, all of which had the unique property of collecting light from all sources, even from distant stars, which could be concentrated inside the interior of the crystal and emitted in any direction in a narrow but very intense beam.

When Atlanteans began to use this crystal as a weapon, their civilization was destroyed. Humanity is now on the verge of rediscovering these crystals.

If we are unable to direct our states, of what use is it to evolve as a Higher Being? Mentation is just one example of many possible disciplines we may acquire in order to direct our new states of Being, especially in our new life in the higher dimensions.

The headbrain as the thinking centrum can only suggest a line of activity and then easily lose it because the thinking centrum has no authority. It lacks the force of will. The higher mental centrum in the tailbrain has the authority to originate and continue mentation for any period until the process is complete.

Contrary to our most cherished beliefs about our intellectual powers, the headbrain does not originate thoughts.

Imagine a gigantic thought-radio transmitting tower. Now imagine all humans participating together in collecting and sorting through the thoughts emanating from this source of all thought. The headbrain captures only one or two thoughts in seventy-thousand, reverberating them slowly, for a duration of seconds, minutes and sometimes even hours, at a time.

Depending on type, we may fall subject to one thought which reverberates as a major theme, then catch a second which reverberates as a secondary theme, then a third which reverberates as a tertiary theme, and then weave these together into the orchestration of what humans of this little planet call *thought*.

The definition of mentation is the focusing of voluntary thoughts falling in a certain category of thought and *only* in that category of thought.

Personality can have many states at once because each part of personality is buffered from the other parts, but Being—because it has unity—can only have one state at a time. This should provide a major clue for us about the difference between the human biological machine and the Being, the non-phenomenal self.

The momentary state of the machine we can call "the average of all possible states" because all possible states are continuously proceeding within the machine simultaneously, just as is its automatic flow of dreams, but in almost complete isolation from one another, at any given moment. The combined average in this case means simply a totality of blending of inner forces such as they happen to occur.

With collected attention we have only one state at any given moment, but this state can change. Now, perhaps, we can catch a glimpse of our own possible future as a Being. The direction of states of Being is the goal of all personal work.

"State" means the full potential of a moment, the whole scale of our present cosmic attention.

Mentation is a transspace ship which can transport us from one ordinary state to another, while mood can take us from a lower state to a higher if we know how to fly it.

Few vehicles exist which can actually convey us from lower to higher dimensions, and the mental can only take us from place to place within a single lower organic octave, or convey us in fantasy to our subjective idea of a higher dimension.

Mentation is to the Work what the monkey wrench is to a mechanic. It is the basis for something which can later become an almost universal tool.

Collected attention is our ticket on the transspace ship in which we will enter into very deep mentation on the question of conscience, which we will call the Holy Planet *Purgatory*. This exercise was also called in past times, "the Dark Night of the Soul".

To be able to rise again from our voluntary exile in this state of deep mentation which places us in temporary exile on the Holy Planet *Purgatory*, we must use an entirely different transspace ship, which happens to require exactly one year and one day to construct and, in addition, can only be constructed on the actual surface of the Holy Planet *Purgatory*.

We must never actually dare to land on the Holy Planet *Purgatory* until we know that we are definitely able to return from exile, which is to say, we are able to complete the process of deep contemplation on the question of conscience and, without the artificial exertion of personal will to do so, emerge from the depths of deep mentation.

The Holy Planet *Purgatory* has two other names, which are **Remorse-of-Conscience** and **The Cave**.

But do you happen to also know the two private names for the Solar-Absolute? They are:

Having-A-Wonderful-Time-Wish-You-Were-Here
and
I-Am, But-I-Forget-Just-What!

E.J. Gold, *En Balance*, Pastel,
10" x 12-1/2", Sennelier, 1973.

CHAPTER ELEVEN

CENTRUM OF GRAVITY QUESTION

A centrum of gravity question is an essential question which we use to create slight discomfort, to keep ourselves off-balance in relation to the machine's ordinary mechanical state of self-oblivion.

We can make any question our temporary centrum-of-gravity until the machine awakens just by sheer agitation; but to make a question a working centrum of gravity, it must be an essential question, one that really is important to us, so our thirst cannot be easily quenched.

This can work for us in the awakening of the machine only if we do not fall asleep in the mechanical satisfaction of easy answers, especially answers from those whom we automatically admire because we believe they know more than we do, probably because they intentionally gave us that impression by the use of clothing, atmospheric setting, and worshipful underlings.

To really make a question mean more than just monkey-curiosity we must not seek a quick end to our restless inquiry.

If we can allow the machine to remain in the severe discomfort of the interior perturbations resulting from the unsettling disturbances which automatically arise from deep, serious questioning, even perhaps losing a night or two of sound sleep, we can use a question to keep the machine slightly off-balance in relation to our ordinary complacent state, which sometimes results in a partial awakening of the machine.

If we can use this process of deep questioning to penetrate the surface of the machine's mental apparatus, we can reach the deeper, more primitive levels of the machine, as indicated by the disturbances produced by the questioning.

Serious questioning of a particular type, along with exact efforts to awaken the machine, will result in interior perturbations which show us that the machine is definitely protecting something which it does not want us to see.

This penetration into the deepest levels of the machine, into the very flesh and blood of the machine, so to speak, can eventually produce the result such that the machine aligns itself to our higher aspirations.

When the machine is in agreement with the higher aspirations, which can only be the result of the mental centrum operating in the tailbrain apparatus, we say that the machine has become purified or, as it was said by the first schools in ancient civilizations, we have become virtuous, meaning that the machine truthfully reflects the higher aims and aspirations.

Paste your centrum of gravity question on your forehead and carry it with you wherever you go, seeing, speaking and listening only in relation to this question.

Make this question your temporary inner god. Not only will this produce something for your later life, but it will also give your actual inner-evil-god a much deserved holiday.

Although this seems like a small exercise, someday you may wonder about things on a much larger scale and having performed this beginning exercise successfully, you will then be able to exert the will to keep those questions alive until they have been answered to your complete satisfaction.

Some questions can be suggested, while others you must discover for yourselves. For example, have you never wondered what happens to stars during the day?

For contemporary science this has an easy answer: stars always are present but in daytime because of atmospheric light we cannot see them.

But your wonderful contemporary science has not yet answered the questions, *What becomes of dreams during the day?* and, *If dreams are continuous even during man's ordinary waking state, what influence do the unknown and ordinarily invisible thoughts, sensations, involuntary spasmodic movements and moods of these continuous dreams exert on the ordinary waking state of the human biological machine?*

I could suggest other questions; for instance, *What is the difference between the memory of actual objective events and continuous dreams for the ordinary human biological machine if it has no unity?*

And another: *Exactly how can artificially produced abrasive outer events produce a definite and exact awakening of the machine which in turn produces an exact change in Being?*

What does it mean to sacrifice the suffering of the machine?

Who exactly within us desires change and what kind of change is really wished for?

What in us really needs change, if anything? How can we force change if there is no necessity? What is the alternative to the way we are now?

Have we ever met any real men, men not in quotation marks? How could we recognize such a man if we did meet him?

What occurs within us that does not "just happen by itself"?

Why is it necessary "to know the human biological machine exactly and intimately"?

How is it possible for us to become responsible for the actions of our own biological machines?

Have we ever really produced just one completely original thought, a thought which originated with us? Can we possibly do this without simply synthesizing results of our conditioning?

Why is it necessary to "force destiny"? Why can't we just wait for our evolution to happen by itself?

What, exactly, is the meaning of "redemption"? What is it that can "suffer redemption"?

How can a permanent identity become fixated? How can we be sure we do not crystallize ourselves in a higher dimension before we achieve the highest possible evolution as individuals?

Even if we knew how to accumulate higher substances, how could we create the necessity for higher bodies?

What influence does our conditioning have on our attitudes, decisions, moods, ability to be receptive to new ideas, etc.?

If we know nothing about The Work, much less how to get ourselves accepted into it, how do we know we want this for ourselves?

What does it mean, "to re-invent oneself"? How can we do this? Of what real use is it for our higher lives?

If the operation of centrums is like a "one-armed bandit", a slot machine in a gambling casino, what makes the organic centrums spin? What makes them stop spinning? What combinations of centrums are possible? Is there a way to use this data for our work to awaken the machine?

What does it mean to "catch oneself red-handed"? Does this relate to the use of small habits as cattle-prods? How can we do this for ourselves, independently of outside help?

How can we become receptive to forces from above? Are all forces from above necessarily for the good?

What personal stakes do we each have for choosing this path? What if we are wrong...what then? How committed are we to remaining in it?

Suppose after all our efforts we still "die like dogs"?

Does the Absolute really suffer? How could we possibly work to alleviate this suffering, if it is true?

How can we make ourselves useful to higher beings, or "Laws"? Are there really such beings? Why do they need such as we?

Why must our work be performed invisibly under ordinary life conditions?

What does "exile" or "separation" mean? What feelings does this evoke, if any? How can we learn to become aware of this feeling?

Why must we struggle to overcome the will of the machine? What other kind of will can there be for us? How can we develop this other will in ourselves?

What exactly is the difference between "sensing" and "feeling"?

What exactly is the difference between "attention" and "awareness"?

Why is gratitude a necessity in work? To whom or what should we feel gratitude? Why?

What is the real meaning and use of worship? What is our place in worship? Are we really the only creature capable of worship? Why is our worship useful to the alleviation of the suffering of the Absolute?

What is the value of gesture, expression and posture in the study of the inner and outer life of the machine? Where do these motor centrum activities come from originally and where are they stored? What is it that activates them? Can they be changed? Should they be changed?

What is silence? Can there ever be complete silence? How can we experience this silence?

What is a real wish? How can it be activated and used in our work?

What is the importance of hospitality in the Work? How can we ever hope to discover its laws and customs if they have been lost in contemporary civilization?

Of what importance is humor in the Work? How can we be sure we really have a sense of humor and not just more automatic defenses of the machine?

Is there any objective use for personal surrender? To what or whom ought we to surrender if there is?

What conditions are necessary before we can be accepted into the Work?

What does it mean for our work that the Absolute is isolated from the moment of Creation? How can this be possible that, "the moment of Creation is the Absolute's only Act of Will"?

We assume that we are alive, yet books such as the Bardo Thodol, commonly called the Tibetan Book of The Dead, are directed at us, not at some ghost hovering around in space. How can we prove to ourselves once and for all that we are in fact alive...if, indeed, we really are alive, as we assume...?

What might happen if we spent all day tomorrow trying individually with all our wit and all the resourcefulness and intelligence at our disposal, to convince just one other person without the smallest doubt that we are really alive...?

E.J. Gold, *Only Part of the Dragon,*
Pastel/Charcoal, 20" x 26", Sennelier, 1987.

CHAPTER TWELVE

SENSING

Through sensing we can follow the momentary concentrations of forces in our organisms, where inner tensions of forces occur, when they shift and at what tempo.

Sensing is very important to us in our work with the machine and, if we hope to be able to awaken the machine, determining its state by its sensations, we must know the definite difference between sensing and feeling.

Sensing can be understood if we can learn to see the inner tensions of the machine, when they shift, and at what tempo. We are not interested in muscular tensions, but in tensions of the electrical forces proceeding in the machine quite apart from its own organic functions.

To follow and be able to use these inner concentrations of force, because we are not taught this
observation from birth, we must learn a new way of
seeing the inner activities of the machine.

Tension collects itself in the organism according
to the laws of the octave, manifesting in any given
place only momentarily.

If we know where tension will next appear we
can expect it and focus our attention before it disap-
pears.

Tension is much quicker than our ability to per-
ceive it and so we must know beforehand where to
look for it.

In this effort an inanimate helper such as prayer
beads or a special rosary can help, following the
formula *one-and-four, four-and-two, two-and-eight,
eight-and-five, five-and-seven, and back full circle to the
tension of forces represented as seven-and-one,* representing the tension between any of two points in the
organism.

In the desert, if we know that big ridges always
lie across the wind, we can make adjustments in our
orientation according to this fact.

Only a very big storm can change the dunes and
one cannot go far during a storm. It is important for
us, if we really wish to work to awaken the machine,
to know this big secret; once in the desert we cannot
depend on ordinary navigation to tell left from right.

When we sense, we do so with the whole attention, so much so that, for the moment, nothing exists
for us except the sensation upon which the attention
is fixated.

When we take a sip of water in this way we do not at the same time allow the attention to wander off in side thoughts of what we had for lunch.

In ordinary life we cannot remember to awaken the machine because at first, when we do not yet know exactly how to awaken it, we try to awaken the machine with mental exertion.

One must learn to distinguish between thinking, feeling and sensing, and then use all three in work.

All experiments with the awakening of the machine require a sustained inner sensing of machine-tensions. Sensing can also be said to be the method of making contact with the inner world by directing at least part of our attention to inner electrical tensions and at the same time sensing the results of these tensions.

Posture evokes mood. We can use this special form of organic suggestibility to remember to awaken the machine by keeping the attention on organic tensions.

Think of the human biological machine as a pinball machine which has lights and bells which activate when they are struck by our attention, represented by the steel ball.

Imagine this pinball machine to have only seven lights, each of a different color and in a different location in the body, each of which also has a corresponding bell, each tuned to a different unique pitch.

Now when the tension shifts from one part of the organism to another, see the bulbs of the two points between which the tension has temporarily come to rest as glowing colored lights, and hear the corresponding bell as it also rings.

Each part activates according to the law of the octave.

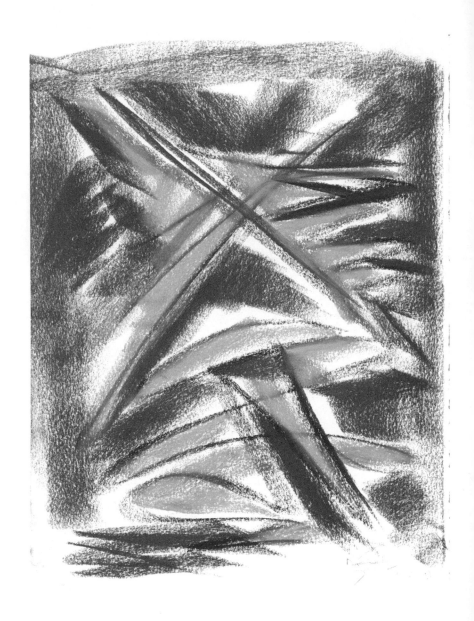

E.J. Gold, *Across the Maze,* Pastel,
11" x 15", Rives BFK, 1987.

CHAPTER THIRTEEN

THINKING BY FORM

A Being who has fallen into identification with the sleep of the machine is forced to involuntarily accept impressions from every source. Impartial man is able to categorically select impressions.

Most of us are able to read and not only able to read; we can be said to be "involuntary readers" in the sense that the machine reads and records mentally everything we see and hear whether we wish it to or not.

This habitual automatic reading of everything we see in written form makes us an involuntary slave to every literary and semi-literary idea which blows across our faces.

We should be able to learn to disallow the automatic associations of the emotional part of the mental apparatus to collect and categorize these impressions upon which the machine's eyes happen to fall.

We should also be able to do the same with objects and verbal sounds, then with sounds of every kind and finally with sensations, until these can all be understood as new and uncategorical impressions.

In this way we can see them in completely new categories beyond the usual habitual patterns.

Observe as impartially as is possible for you presently how this involuntary acceptance of impressions, particularly of the written word, makes real understanding impossible.

The ordinary involuntary but literate human being is blind to just how his impressions are categorized because he is forced to continually rely on habit.

The lower centrums of the machine are just too slow to follow and direct these inner psychological processes.

We assume that we understand all the things we read, see, and hear because they evoke in the machine those automatic associations which seem, for some unaccountable reason, somehow familiar, and therefore beyond question.

Whenever common sense permits, you can try an experiment: become an "intentional illiterate" who is, for some unexplained reason, suddenly unable to understand the written word.

Do not hide your involuntary illiteracy beneath confusion, just void your habit of automatically decoding, understanding and categorizing the written word and allowing it, without authorization, to become a permanent entry in the lower mental apparatus.

E.J. Gold, *Figure with Crutch*, Charcoal,
22" x 30", Rives BFK, 1987.

CHAPTER FOURTEEN

REMORSE OF CONSCIENCE

The organ "conscience" is in ordinary man atrophied from disuse and isolation. Remorse of conscience can repair our past—no matter what we may have done.

The organ *conscience* is in the ordinary human biological machine completely atrophied as a result of the disuse and isolation caused by the inactive state of the emotional centrum.

This isolation is broken from time to time, either accidentally from some shock, or intentionally by an artificial technique which is called *Remorse of Conscience.*

When the machine's mother dies it feels, perhaps for the very first time ever, although the source of attention may not be aware of it, the automatic arising of the emotion called Remorse of Conscience.

We feel this in the machine because, although in many ways we may have been a good child, at the same time—also in many ways—we must inevitably have failed in our obligation to her for giving the machine life and preparing us, in her own unique or not-so-unique way, for responsible age.

This debt is so great that we could not possibly repay it no matter what, especially in her opinion. This debt to our mother is what can be called "original sin", not some imaginary fall from some imaginary state of Grace. But the machine is a swine of the first degree, and soon forgets this momentary discomfort, and in a few weeks is able to sink back into the usual mechanical oblivion.

We can use these first stirrings of conscience activated by the mood of "remorse" for past wrongdoings and injustices on our part, to provide us with the motivation to conserve our precious time and energy for our work to awaken the machine.

We can use this emotional state to help us remember to spend our inner force and subjective time not just for self-satisfaction, but for work, which alone can give our life in the machine any real meaning.

To activate these deep, essential feelings of remorse in the machine, we should act toward, speak, and respond to everyone we know and meet as if to our own dear mother.

Soon not only will we respond very differently to everyone, more responsibly, but we can also in this way repay our debt to her.

Whether or not she is presently in this world, we can use the sensations of remorse to repair the past in relation to her, and by doing so, begin to make a bridge to our past, in preparation for the awakening of the machine *before we ever heard these ideas,* which we can do only because the Creation contains all events and the past still exists.

If we have also activated the higher emotional centrum, it is possible to use this same exercise on a higher scale to give our mother or our grandmother the means to become a saint, if she had already developed in herself some feelings of objective conscience, but did not have sufficient time in the life of the machine to fully develop this higher impulse.

E.J. Gold, *Temple in the Sky*, Pastel,
14" x 17", Arches, 1987.

CHAPTER FIFTEEN

DOORWAYS

The practice of remembering ourselves, "invoking our presences", having the continual presence of "I" makes a "vibration of Being" which gradually forms a relatively permanent crystallization called "Gradation of Evolution".

The presence of the nonphenomenal source of attention within the awakened machine, because negative emotion is absent in the awakened machine, produces the vibration which gradually forms itself into the permanent crystallization which we call the *Being*.

Each stage of transformation of the Being produced by the awakened machine is called "Gradation of Evolution".

We can separate the process of transformation governed by the human biological machine into twenty-one definite Gradations of Evolution, each slightly more objective than the previous gradation in the sense of existing in higher and higher dimensions as we scale upward toward the Absolute.

Under no circumstance is it possible for us to attain the three highest forms of existence, the highest of which is the Absolute itself, pure Being. No one who knows anything would really wish to evolve to the gradation of the Absolute, and it would be of no benefit to oneself or to the Absolute. Each Gradation of Evolution represents a specific crystallization of the Being. These higher gradations of evolution can only be the results of intentional transformation.

The transference of the identity from the nonphenomenal source of attention to the Being is necessary for the moment of machine-death when it is once again returned to its natural organic source-of-substances.

Even the nonphenomenal source of attention eventually dies if it has existed without transformation, but the Being which has become a permanent crystallization can never die.

Perhaps we ought to first taste what it means never to die...maybe we would prefer to just fall into annihilation and forget everything.

No two Beings have exactly the same frequency of vibration. Frequencies are limited in number because they are, as is everything, material. However, due to a surplus of apathetic humans and a corresponding paucity of transformed Beings, very few frequencies have ever been taken off the market.

The stable Gradation of Evolution several times removed from the ordinary state of a human being, when taken in relation to a successful transference of identity from the nonphenomenal source of attention to the Being, can be called "Objective Consciousness" when developed.

Although we may not understand exactly how this might be true, stepping through a doorway is to taste death in some form. When passing the threshold of a portal, we can use this as a reminding factor to exert our will to awaken the machine. Passing a portal, even in the form of an ordinary door, is like the moment of death, the passing of the portal for which we prepare ourselves all our lives. We practice the awakening of the machine during these little deaths so that at our passing, when the chains of life are thrown off, and we feel our life slipping away, we will have attention, presence, Being, and an unshakeable work-habit.

Only then will we taste of death and not feel its sting.

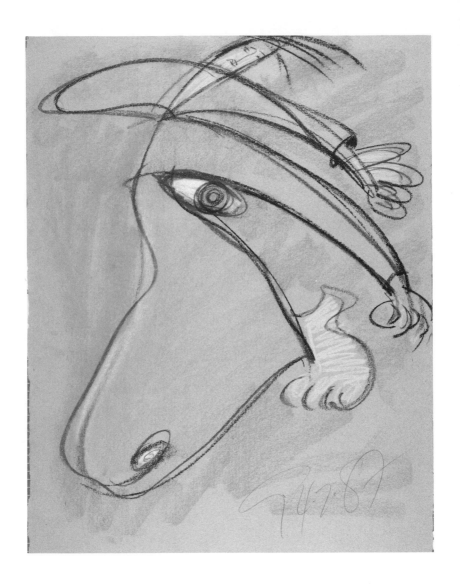

E.J. Gold, *The Donkey in the Village,*
Pastel, 20" x 26", Sennelier, 1987.

CHAPTER SIXTEEN

RED-FACED DONKEY

We have much to gain from manifesting without considering, without fear for self, without desire to protect our vanity and self-love; we must free ourselves from the opinion of others.

Have you ever had the feeling that people in ordinary life seem to be from a different planet or at any rate, are hard to communicate with—that they lack the same feelings, sensitivities to higher aesthetics from which you suffer? Do they seem brutal, apathetic, cruel, at times to be the walking dead, just cold, lifeless self-propelled robotic pieces of flesh?

All the people you know are in automatic sympathy, emotional identification of the mental centrum, with trivial things.

Maybe you find it hard to understand them now, but later on, after you have worked a little to awaken the machine, the distance will seem even greater and more impassable.

If the mainstream of human life is totally focused on trivia, then do we, who hope to prepare ourselves for the Work, know what is not trivia? We should know, because everyone here is slightly higher than ordinary human beings, or at least focused on slightly less popular trivia.

When, exactly, does mere whim become whimsy? Whimsy can, however, be used as a source of peculiarities for some sort of leverage for our efforts in conjunction with the exertion of our will to awaken the machine.

We have two prospects—trivia and whimsy. We must differentiate between them. In the beginning we are all like dull, dry Alice. Later, we may become more like the droll caterpillar or gain the otherworldly wit of the Cheshire Cat. We must never become the time-conscious, neurotic, eager-to-please White Rabbit which is the machine at its worst.

Now we must consider! Just what are we to make trivial? What should we make important?

We could make trivial: Opinions, relationships—for instance, our associate's pecking order—diet, routines, speed or tempo of work, our attachment to various social activities, the machine's automatically generated negative feelings about the manifestations of others or critical feelings about the environment, feelings of personal hurt, self-righteousness, making others wrong, the desire to do whatever we prefer to do upon rising in the morning instead of trying to awaken the machine, the manner of getting out of bed, the feelings of resentment which result from disagreement or disapproval, boredom, the automatic desire to manifest in a particularly sincere or earnest fashion, to appear to others that way.

We could make important: To change the tempo of the machine's actions, to have the hair brushed and neat all day, to have shoes on at all times, even in bed, to make sure to lead with the right foot while going through doorways, or stepping off curbs, to wash the dishes as soon as the meal is over, to dress or undress in a particular order, to read everything twice, to walk around with eggs in the right-hand pocket.

This little exercise is based on the idea that what the machine finds offensive to its vanity will force it to awaken just a little. Whenever possible without really becoming offensive or obnoxious about it, take a totally undefendable, utterly untenable, completely ridiculous position about something, against all rationality, especially at the risk of your personal vanity and reputation as a reasonable and intelligent human being.

This experiment must of course be harmless to oneself and to others, except as it affects the insecurity and fears of the machine expressing themselves in the form of personal vanity.

Maintain this posture just like the red-faced donkey you really are, regardless of how disgusted others become with you, no matter what they call you or how they consider you from then on. Soon you ought to be a total social disaster and a pariah, an outcast.

Do not be a slave to the opinions of others, be free of what others think of you and, in addition, be free of your own opinion of your machine's manifestations. Freedom cannot be purchased like an automobile or a full-length sable coat, although freedom has its price. Suffering inside with this donkeyness is a double-edged sword. The machine cannot be a donkey in the eyes of itself and others, but the Being feels no humiliation.

Be careful when first learning to be an intentional donkey, because the machine has safety valves... suffering can easily become pleasure. The first time the machine feels the pain of rejection it feels hurt, but by the fifth time it actually *likes* to be a donkey, feeling nothing where there was once a little pain.

Dare to manifest without the fear of humiliation. This exercise of intentional humiliation, along with the repair of the heart by following the moving manifestations of the machine during manual labor, and the ascension onto the Cross, the intersection of time and space, by contemplation upon—and psychoemotional identification with—the sensations and emotions of the Man on the Cross, is the Western monk's great secret.

E.J. Gold, *Seeking Refuge*, Charcoal,
22" x 30", Rives BFK, 1987.

CHAPTER SEVENTEEN

CHIEF WEAKNESS

We must see what we ought to do and know the weakness which makes us unable to do it. This weakness is called Chief Feature. We usually think of this weakness as the best and nicest part of ourselves.

Every small effort to awaken the machine is a small act toward the eventual development of the will of the nonphenomcnal self over the will of the machine.

To really suffer intentional Purgatory, we must see what we ought to do, and know the weakness of the machine which makes us unable to do what we should do. This inherent flaw in the machine we can call our *Chief Weakness*. We usually think of this weakness as the best and nicest part of ourselves. The Chief Weakness is only one of the many destructive results of having lived our lives immersed in helpless identification with the sleeping machine.

One factor by which we can recognize our Chief Weakness is that it requires no effort at all to develop it and no special effort to maintain its manifestations.

The Being is born among a sleeping people. Everything in the surroundings is part of the unconscious conspiracy of Great Nature to keep us in sleep so that we will continue to fulfill our part in the cosmic necessity. By the time the machine has reached what would otherwise have been responsible age, responsible in the real sense of the word, we have developed very strong habits of sleep, and very intense efforts are necessary to awaken the machine...that is, if, for us, it is still possible.

Sometimes habits of sleep are so entrenched that nothing can help, not even a powerful higher influence, and our fate is sealed. Much special help is needed if we have developed strong habits of sleep, and it is very expensive in many ways to provide such help. Only for someone who has already made considerable efforts toward awakening and transformation, can it be considered worth the risk and effort.

In our ordinary state, the idea, *gnothe seauton,* "Know Thyself" means nothing, because our education does not prepare us to understand what human life is *for,* and if we do not know our purpose for life in the human biological machine, we cannot possibly suspect that the machine is not functioning as a transformational apparatus.

As ignorant as our ordinary education leaves us, not only do we know nothing about the ordinary uses of the machine as it exists in nature, but we would never in the ordinary course of events, which is to say, without the intentional influence of a school, discover the really unique purpose to which it could be put. Thus only rarely do a few human beings in any generation ever happen to learn about the possibility of *intentional evolution.*

When it comes to protecting itself from observation, the machine is very clever; we will never be able to observe the Chief Weakness if we try to look for it directly. Therefore, we must find a way to observe it indirectly, to observe the traces of its activities, because when the Chief Weakness is active, that is to say, during periods of deep sleep of the machine, our attention is prevented by the machine's density from observing the Chief Weakness actually at work.

A machine must inevitably behave as a machine, think as a machine, feel as a machine, sense as a machine. It can do nothing else and we must make allowances for this or, for a very long time, we will suffer when observing the results left in the wake of the sleeping machine, because we are observing a machine which up to now we have been identifying to ourselves and others as our own "self".

Our Chief Weakness is something we have whether we wish it or not; we cannot just decide it out of existence, and the situation will never improve by the sheer force of mental imagination. If we have learned anything about work, we realize that our Chief Weakness, as with all mechanicalities of the machine, can be an instrument for the awakening of the machine. A weakness is not easy to see and can seldom be shown to us by another. We must observe impartially for a very long time before we can see our own Chief Weakness. Only then, when we see it for ourselves, will we really believe in its existence and power.

We must not be too much in love with the moods, thoughts and sensations of the machine to observe impartially, remembering that it provides these distractions and seductions only for its own smug satisfaction. Our work just begins when we can see exactly what it is that we must struggle against.

But what is our enemy now can also be our greatest ally in the Work. One big part of work is to learn how to turn these involuntary enemies into friends for work.

How can we struggle against our Chief Weakness when it is only active during periods of deep sleep of the machine and is therefore invisible to our observation? We can listen to the machine's thoughts and words as if listening to a stranger speaking on a radio over a long distance. We may be very shocked to hear some of the ideas which spring from the mouth of the machine, but do not reflect our ideas at all.

E.J. Gold, *Manger Scene,* Charcoal,
22" x 30", Rives BFK, 1987.

CHAPTER EIGHTEEN

REPAIRING THE PAST

Out of habit, ordinary man lives in one centrum only. When it is burned out, the centrum dies and becomes useless. At that point, a man can no longer work because he is already one-third dead.

When we are identified with the sleeping machine, we live only in the lower story of our organic house. Out of habit, we use one single centrum until it is useless and then, when it has burned out, we move like a gypsy into another camp. If we lived like this in an ordinary house, we would not bother to replace a lightbulb when it burned out; we would simply move to another room. By the time we are forced to evacuate one centrum and relocate in another centrum, the machine is already one-third dead.

We would prefer to redecorate this new centrum in more or less the same way as our former centrum from which we are now a refugee, but we no longer possess everything we formerly had.

We were forced to leave a great deal behind when we evacuated. In this new centrum we must improvise, make old familiar things with materials which seem very different. But with fantasy and imagination we can make ourselves feel almost as comfortable as we were in our previous habitation.

If we are accustomed to this single-centrumed life, we could go mad as a result of this forced exile from our customary domicile. When all the material for life of this centrum had been used up, we would be forced to move to another centrum, there to become pathological and stupidly repetitive. After this, we would have nowhere else to which we could retreat and our only possible fate would be to await the inevitable organic death of the whole machine.

Even in small children one centrum may be used up at an early age. Each centrum has only so much life depending on impressions, and how it is used. When a centrum is used up, it is almost impossible to repair. Although every human biological machine has more or less the same allotment in the beginning, each uses this material for life at a different tempo.

In ordinary life it would be our fate to die first in one centrum, then in another, and finally in a third, the death of each centrum signaling the onset of mysterious new illnesses which are called by scientists of contemporary medicine, "civilization diseases". Nothing available in the course of ordinary events would prevent this inexorable disintegration.

When one centrum dies, the machine can no longer function as a transformational apparatus, and we are constrained to send those away who are dead in one or more centrums, unless they are useful to our work as a community.

Sometimes it is possible to use a special ancient Sumerian method, what the Essenes living near Alexandria called "raising the dead". We may, if the necessity arises, be able to repair a machine which is beyond ordinary hope. But this is so expensive that we cannot do it unless we have help from the higher dimensions, which means that it is somehow profitable for the work of higher dimensions. For any hope of possible evolution, the machine must be not only awake, but whole, its centrums intact and functional.

If we had only three pair of shoes in our whole life, and could never replace them, we would be fools to wear only one pair until it wore out and then wear another, and then the third pair. If we know how to live, we will change our shoes often, use them equally, make them last longer.

It is not enough to begin now to live in more than just one centrum. Already we have wasted precious time by restricting our life and attention to only one centrum. Now we must not only repair the present, but also repair the past. We can repair the past to some extent by reviewing the life of the machine—at least its most important points— through the colored lenses of those centrums we ordinarily do not use.

Our three-centrum review of the life of the machine conforms to the *Law of Catching Up*. Thanks to our past identification with one dominant centrum of the sleeping machine, we already know quite enough about the other reciprocal law, the *Law of Falling.*

At the end of each day, review impartially everything you did, along with everything that happened to you, but do not review these in the ordinary way.

You are to make three separate and distinct passes through these events, reviewing each event through one of the three main lenses: sensing, feeling and thinking, one lens at a time.

For the purpose of this exercise, you should keep three separate journals, one for each centrum, each journal in the subjective language of its own unique centrum.

E.J. Gold, *Dancing in the Rain,*
Pastel, 11" x 15", Rives BFK, 1987.

CHAPTER NINETEEN

WALKING BETWEEN RAINDROPS

Posture is mother to mood; tempo of work is mother to organic and psychic tempo; self-initiated voluntary manifestation is mother to death with presence.

There is a song that talks about walking between the raindrops. We can use this same idea, walking between the raindrops of our customary motor centrum postures, gestures and facial expressions, to help us gain the will to awaken the machine, if we have studied the machine and are able to recognize our customary postures just before they are about to appear.

Even without will over the machine, we can suggest slight adjustments in the machine to avoid these habitual postures *if we can convince the machine that they make it look ugly.*

It is not necessary to look like a complete idiot to others just to perform this exercise. The variance between customary postures, gestures and expressions and those "between-raindrops" alternates should be so subtle that they are completely invisible to a casual observer.

We must consider the possible effect upon others when making this experiment; it is unlawful to work on ourselves at the expense of others.

View those postures which you have determined are customary for the machine as your enemies, into which you must not fall even momentarily. Do anything necessary, even throw the machine off balance, to avoid sinking into these "resting places". Jump, walk in a zig-zag, dodge and twist like a football player, as if walking between raindrops. If your attention is distracted, begin again.

Habitual postures of the motor centrum can be present in the form of utterances, expressions of the facial mask, hand gestures, rolling of eyeballs heavenward.

Every motor centrum habit-of-manifestation gives us a small warning signal in the sensing centrum when it is about to become active. We can easily become sensitive to these warning signals; this is not a very advanced exercise, and even a green beginner can do it fairly well.

When this exercise is going well, add to it several mental and emotional postures of the machine.

E.J. Gold, *Games in Light and Dark,*
Charcoal, 11" x 15", Rives BFK, 1987.

CHAPTER TWENTY

CENTRUM OF COSMOS

Man has no real place in the cosmic octave. He is nothing and less than nothing in the big scheme of things, but he has significance in another octave not concentrated in the Great Cosmic Octave.

Alone we can easily visualize the human biological machine as the Solar-Absolute, the Crown of Creation, or as the moon, a new formation at the tail end of the Scale of Creation.

But with others, we can never see the machine as the Solar-Absolute, because of the tensions, emanations and radiations of others, and at the same time the machine's automatic tensions in relation to the machines of others.

The Descending Scale of Creation can be a tool for understanding more than just the theory of astronomy.

Creation was not slowly made over a long period of time. As a matter of fact, the Creation did not appear in time. It *is* time... exactly one moment, which in the objective sense is the same thing as saying eternity.

Everything which exists within the Creation exists eternally in its own time and place. Once existing, always existing, because the Creation is not a flow of events but a living, eternal mathematical equation, expressing itself as matter, which is energy viewed below the speed of light, and energy, which is matter viewed at or above the speed of light.

In a way, the Creation is an eternal light in infinite extension, folded in upon itself in the form of a Klein Bottle, a solid form of the Moebius Strip.

Time is the unique subjective through which we are able to thread our way through the space of higher dimensions and view time as a lower dimension.

All lower worlds are only temporary, except for organic life in general. In the life of planets and suns there is no question of evolution; they all will someday be higher...But for moons, new Beings formed of negative energy, there can be no guarantee and the risk of annihilation is great.

What do you think it might mean, to feed the moon in oneself? Without this internal moon, the machine cannot attain the imbalance and disharmony necessary to function as a transformational apparatus.

Man has no real place in the higher dimensions of the Cosmic Octave; he is nothing and less than nothing in the big scheme of things, but he has significance in another octave not evident within the Great Cosmic Octave. It is in this hidden octave that he can try to become more than is possible for him in the ordinary course of evolution.

In studying the law of octaves it must be remembered that octaves in relation to one another are divided into fundamental and subordinate octaves. Retardations can in this way be understood as potentials of new directions. We can never learn to use fully the laws of octaves, but we can learn to use some of its laws.

While the Being is under the Law of Three, the machine is inexorably under the Law of Seven. If we really understand this idea, we have a very powerful tool for work. It would be beneficial in this respect to study deeply the laws of the octave.

Parables are the speech of conscious Beings, blended for multi-dimensional significance, to conform to their vision of life as they see, hear, feel, sense and understand it.

Choose an object and make it temporarily represent for you the Solar-Absolute; for the purpose of this experiment, every other object and being in the cosmos exists only subordinately in relation to it.

Now visualize all those objects, events and ideas which, from the very beginning of time to the extreme end, were and are necessary for its appearance, continued existence, maintenance and appreciation.

Extend your vision throughout all Creation, permeating all Being and manifestation in order to fully see everything necessary to maintain the existence of this single object which is the centrum of gravity of the entire Creation.

It is not necessary to have the object constantly in sight. Go about your daily business, considering how everything in the universe supports the existence of this single object.

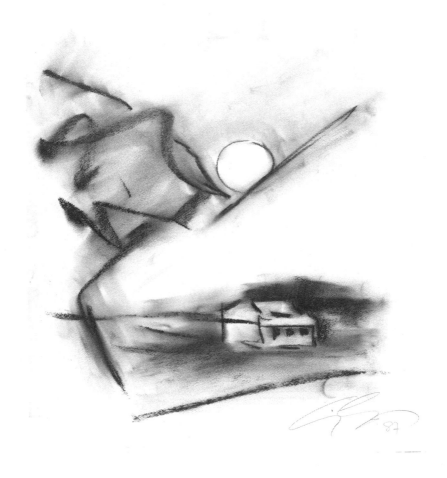

E.J. Gold, *Impression Sunrise Barstow,*
Pastel, 14" x 17", Arches, 1987.

CHAPTER TWENTY-ONE

NEW DAY EVERY DAY

The machine has the disease of "tomorrow". Tomorrow is the only day which—just perhaps— could be that not-quite-attainable day of "roses, roses". In work, however, we can take nothing for granted.

We can quite easily accept ordinary sleep and surrender to it without too much struggle when we are young. Later in life, the machine resists even ordinary sleep, but not nearly as much as it resists death.

We can persuade the machine to surrender to ordinary sleep because the machine is reasonably certain that tomorrow it will open its eyes and find everything more or less the same as it was today. If everything remains rational and predictable, even if miserable, then the machine will not, unless something very unexpected happens to disturb its usual smug somnambulance, become too upset.

Animals do not make a distinction between sleep and death. The human biological machine among all creatures of organic life resists death. Animals may struggle against an enemy, or to escape a trap, but they will never resist a quiet death.

If the human biological machine knows that it will die soon, its mental centrum will begin to consider very differently about tomorrow. The machine will have a strong desire to live even one more hour, and hopefully even one more day, unless it is in very bad pain.

The machine has the "disease of tomorrow". Tomorrow just perhaps could be that not quite attainable day of nonstop absence of pain, even if today was thorns and yesterday was shit. Death, no matter when it comes, will always seem to the machine to come at just the wrong moment, just when everything is about to go right. Death cheats the machine of this hope. It is a special sleep from which the machine is sure it will never wake up. Death can come at any time but most easily and without our notice at night.

Each day the machine happens to live on is due mostly to blind luck. So many things can happen... If we should happen to wake up in the machine tomorrow morning, we should, at the first glimpse of a new day, fall on our knees with gratitude for another chance to accomplish what we failed to accomplish with the machine yesterday.

Maybe we will have a whole day to work on self, maybe only the time to brush our hair and comb our teeth.

Each night as we lay down with the machine, we should strive to see sleep as a kind of death, understanding that there exists a very real possibility that we may *not* for one reason or another awaken in the morning.

If we enter deep sleep voluntarily, allowing this little idea to continue during the night, and it happens not to influence our ultra-suggestible machines into an immediate termination of life, then we ought, at the dawn of a new day, to feel the impulse of real gratitude, for the possibility for work presented by an additional day of life.

When we wake in the morning, besides jumping out of bed like a jungle animal, eyes open and at full all-centrums-alert, we should spend the first five minutes doing nothing but trying to awaken the machine.

Then we should form the idea in our mental centrum that we have awakened in a new world; we must not assume that what we see today is the same as what we saw yesterday; people and things we think we recognize may not be exactly the same today as they were the day before.

In this life, we must take nothing for granted. We cannot assume that just because our surroundings seem familiar, they have any relation to what we learned about our outer world yesterday. Not only will everyone's state be different, but in a real way everything will be different, just like a New World.

Even when looking into a mirror, and maybe especially then, we are sure to see a total stranger to what we were yesterday. We must be very careful to observe the machine and everything else with new eyes as if seeing a new world for the very first time. For now we are not interested in every little detail of this New World, only in its most gross manifestations. Later with practice we will see much more.

In this experiment we must try to see ourselves as a complete stranger to the machine and to this world, exiled from our familiar surroundings, living a life totally uncustomary to our habitual experience.

We can observe, making no assumptions that we understand what we see, knowing nothing about the significance-of-it-all.

We must learn to think, feel and sense ourselves in exile from the planet "Yesterday" with only the vague possibility of arriving at the planet "Today", where we are like newborns who know nothing of what may be in store for us.

Too often do we mistake one word for a similar word, one object for another like it, and one person for someone else just because they have similar features. We often make someone pay for something another did just because they remind us vaguely of someone who wronged us in the past but is now not available for the possible expression of our revenge.

Even when waking in the morning and seeing those we take as our ordinary friends and family we can try to see that they are not the same as those of yesterday, even in the ordinary sense. Every day we are really in a strange land among strangers we do not know and cannot completely know, for today they are not what they were yesterday and we cannot depend on them to be the same.

We must rearrange our idea of the world to see that each new day is really a new world and that those things which appear the same really are not the same.

E.J. Gold, *And Where is the Dog?*,
Pastel, 10" x 12-1/2", Sennelier, 1987.

CHAPTER TWENTY-TWO

"I" CAN DO ANYTHING

Whereas I can do anything, the machine is a congenital bungler.

If we recognize our present state, we must inevitably feel the urgency to work toward the awakening of the machine and toward our own transformation.

We know that we are at war, and we know the enemy; it is our own complacency, our own willingness to be carried along by the sleep of the machine. But once we decide to work, we must accept everything that comes to us in the way of work.

Most importantly, we must learn to make decisions rapidly; if we are offered a work-task, it is vital that we accept the task *immediately* and without hesitation.

We soon learn, if we remain in the work-community long enough to learn anything, that if we hesitate even momentarily, the offer is withdrawn and may never be offered again. In this work, hesitation, suspicion, negativity, argument, fear, insecurity, sarcasm and smart-ass cynicism are taken to indicate that in our minds, *we have already failed the task*.

It must be quite clear in our minds that if we refuse work, we refuse help. We must understand that it is *sleep* which is our enemy, *not those who prepare us for evolution.*

Pretend that you have discovered some substance which we will call *Luckium*. Whenever you carry this "Luckium" in your pocket or as a charm on a chain around your neck you feel absurdly, even stupidly, optimistic about everything, estimating your abilities and willingness far beyond your ordinary limits.

While you carry this substance Luckium around with you, you feel wonderful, and very lucky. You have supreme confidence in yourself, and whenever anyone asks you to perform a task, without considering once—or even pausing for reflection, except in consideration of your actual organic safety—you immediately express abject glee, agreeing immediately and unquestioningly to perform the task regardless of any dislike you may have toward it.

You should cheerfully grin like a village idiot, and reply, "Sure! I can do *anything!*" Just be sure when you say this that *I* is really speaking, because, while *I* really *can* do anything, the machine happens to be a congenital bungler. This "insane optimism" and amiable willingness to do almost anything at all should soon make us very popular among our lazy friends.

E.J. Gold, *You'll Never Believe What Just Happened*,
Pastel, 10" x 12-1/2", Sennelier, 1987.

CHAPTER TWENTY-THREE

RADIATION OF PAIN

Sensations of pain and pleasure can be used as reminding factors; they can provide the force for the awakening of the machine.

Pain and discomfort can be used as an exercise. First we must lessen their intensity, by extending them outward.

Slowly, using the attention and concentration of half of the attention, radiate the pain outward into neighboring cells.

As the pain radiates outward, you will notice that the intensity of the sensation seems to dissolve slightly, like salt in water.

If you add no additional salt, you can radiate pain throughout the machine without causing an imbalance elsewhere as a result. Even slight discomfort such as an itching sensation can be radiated in this way, providing the force for the awakening of the machine.

In the past, when these small organic pains occurring automatically in the machine had no purpose for our work to awaken the machine, we wished at all costs to be rid of them.

Now, perhaps you can see how small, relatively unimportant pains can help you in your work, by providing your attention with a specific field of gravitational attraction.

A strong or unusual sensation in the machine can become a tiny Sun-Absolute from which radiates the force for attention to follow sensation through the machine.

We can also use sensations which happen to be pleasurable to the machine, because sensations of pleasure and sensations of pain are exactly the same, except in the matter of their specific intensity. In addition, we could use our pains to awaken the machine by following this method:

First, we must keep in mind that the machine is asleep and that its sleep is like the sleep of a limb, an arm or a leg, in the sense that it becomes numb. We must then remember what it feels like when the limb awakens. We begin to feel sharp, uncomfortable sensations which we commonly call "pins-and-needles".

Hold this idea while at the same time concentrating on the pains ordinarily proceeding in the machine. Get the idea that these are the same sensations which would occur if a limb had fallen asleep. See and feel these sensations at the same time holding firmly the idea that part of the machine is waking up. Encourage these sensations, because they can bring on the sensations of awakening.

Any unpleasant sensation at all will serve this function, but particularly one which is characterized by a tingling reminiscent of the discomfort first felt when a limb has fallen asleep.

As the sensation is magnified by the attention, feel the progressive awakening of the machine.

In this way we use sensations of pain to represent the awakening of the machine, and in this way prepare ourselves for the real sensations of awakening when they do come.

The sensations of awakening are nothing to be afraid of; just a natural and harmless process which is not particularly pleasant, but if we do not fall back into sleep to avoid the discomfort, these unpleasant sensations soon pass and the machine will naturally awaken.

The whole world may seem sluggish and dead as we begin to sense the machine's sleep, but we must find the courage to continue through the strange sensations, the fears, the apprehensions, the anxieties which may arise. All this is perfectly normal; after all, we are so accustomed to the numbing anesthetic of sleep!

Allow yourself to feel anxious, admit to yourself that you feel frightened, anxious, even revolted at the idea of finding yourself in a dead body.

These first feelings will pass. If we allow ourselves to backslide, it will be ten times harder to approach it again.

So be brave, be courageous. You will experience your imprisonment in a dead body, but soon the dead body will begin to awaken. Then the situation will take a new turn; people around you will seem dead—but not everybody—as you look around, you will see some whose eyes are a little bit open or very much open. Work with your pains, using them to reawaken the circulation in this lifeless body, this sleeping machine.

E.J. Gold, *The Golden Age,*
Charcoal, 11" x 15", 1987.

CHAPTER TWENTY-FOUR

LAST HOUR OF LIFE

To know how to settle accounts every hour is something every man should have learned in school, just as to learn to breathe, to eat, to move, and to awaken the machine should be part of any genuine curriculum of education.

How would you like to discover just how precious life really is, but only in your last moment, just as the machine is taking its last few breaths? What would you learn about life? What would you appreciate suddenly, that you had never really appreciated—maybe never even noticed—before this moment?

Above everything else would be breath. Perhaps for the first time, you would notice that every in-breath was accompanied by smells!·

And what exquisite smells! Suddenly you cling to the experience of every aroma. You notice that each scent is a combination of many different tones, and you may even be able, for the first time in your life—and also the last—to be able to separate and identify many of the individual tones and overtones which combine to produce what we call an olfactory chord.

Next, you may come to notice the physical sensations of the machine, and even though many of them may be painful, some will suggest by association all those wonderful experiences of the past which suddenly seem so precious.

Every movement of the machine may be its last, and you may be struck by the beauty of machine-sensations, your attention following each movement and involuntary reflex of the body intensely, thirstily, as a lover follows even the smallest movements of the beloved.

You may think to yourself, "This is a fine time to begin *this* exercise!", but now there is nothing you can do to make up for your past lack of will or enthusiasm before you became aware that the body was actually dying.

Why, suddenly, has life become so very precious? Why does your attention cling to every micro-movement and every sight, smell, sound, and sensation? Why does your brain recount with nostalgia all the main events of the life of the machine? Why, suddenly, is everything you have failed to do in life important to you, even though there is nothing you can do about it now?

What is it that has really changed? You knew all along that someday the machine would die. Why was this knowledge not sufficient to provide you with the motivation to exert your will to awaken over the will of the machine to remain asleep?

Why was it not enough to make you appreciate life *to this extent:* that just the mechanics of bodily survival and the passage of time, which before this seemed to drag on interminably and now rushes by inexorably, can be easily followed in detail by your attention, as if you had just now suddenly discovered a treasure you had never known existed. Yet you had it all the time!

Can you explain to yourself why, although you were told about this years ago, you failed to treat every breath, every movement, every sensation, every smell, every sight, every relationship, every activity as if it were the treasure it is now, at this moment, as you lie here dying?

Now suppose that you somehow learned that you had exactly one hour to live. What would you do with this last precious hour on Earth? If you could use this last hour of life to complete all your business with the machine and with the organic world, would you understand how to do this? Would you be satisfied, at your last breath, that you had really done everything possible in life to complete your life to your own Being-satisfaction?

Not only is this last hour the most important hour of your life at this moment; it sets the scene for the final impressions received by the Being through the machine.

How fragile organic life really is! At any moment the machine is only a hair's-breadth away from death. From the first moment of conception, we live on borrowed time.

In order to really have the freedom to live, we must settle all our business before we die, even in the final hour of life if necessary. But...how do we know exactly which hour will be our last? To be absolutely safe, we should settle our accounts with nature and with the machine at the beginning of each hour, then death can never catch us by surprise.

Exactly how to settle accounts every hour is something every human being should have learned in grade school, along with breathing, eating, moving, invocation of presence and the awakening of objective conscience. One thing we can ask ourselves is who would be hurt by our death if we died in our present condition.

At the moment of death we should have presence, a clear mind and conscience, taking our last breath with the definite satisfaction that we have done everything within our power to fully use our life.

Day by day, if we should ever take the trouble to look, we will discover things which have been left undone and which are in need of repair. It is a mark of a real human being who has really lived that he has squeezed from life every possible drop of quality. We should strive to live our life so that one day we can say at any moment, "Today, I can die without regret."

Never waste what might very well be for you your last hour of life. No matter how long you live, this last hour will be for you the most important. If you do badly at your last hour, you will certainly feel the sensation of regret. This sensation—if you can allow yourself to feel it now—can be a powerful motivating force to prepare yourself for a clean passage out of the machine. If you knew for a fact that this hour were really your last, you would eat impressions as if they were gourmet food. A real connoisseur of life knows how to extract from every morsel of life the last drop of quality.

Demand quality in everything; do not live life as a savage.

During the last hour of your life, you may not have a choice over where you are, or with whom, but you do definitely have a choice over the *quality* of the time, because it is you—and you alone—who determine the state of the machine, whether it is alive or dead, at any moment, including the last.

The extraction of the essential qualities from life utilizes the same technique as the extraction of higher substances from food, air and impressions, which is to say, it is automatically accomplished by the awakening of the machine. If you wish real quality from life, your life must be given up to the Work for the greater good. For just your personal self, you can have very little. Working toward transformation of your Being not for your own benefit but for the benefit of the Absolute, which is the same thing as saying for all Beings everywhere, is an effective technique for evolution.

If you are not satisfied with the quality of your last hour of life, you will not be satisfied with your life as a whole.

To die is to move past something that will never come again in exactly the same way. All great philosophers practiced for their last hour of life. I will give you the same exact exercise which they used to practice for their final hour on Earth. Take care not to change even one word of this instruction:

Look back at the last hour which has just passed as if it had been your final hour on Earth, and you have just now realized that you have died.

First, ask yourself if you are satisfied with how you have used this last precious hour of life.

Now return to the stream of organic life and set yourself the aim during the next hour—if you live that long—to extract just a little more quality from life than you had during the previous hour.

Determine to awaken the machine just a little more, to have just a little more presence in the present, a little more inner fire.

Now open your eyes a little wider; by this I mean awaken the machine and bathe in its transformational effects...be a little more brave than you were for the past hour. You can afford to have courage now that you know it is your last hour and you have nothing to lose. Of course don't be foolishly so.

Know yourself a little more; see your machine just a little more impartially. Now that you are dying, there is no point defending the machine's personal vanity, is there?

Every hour, from now on until your real final hour, demand from the machine, by its awakening, more quality of life, more life in the intuitive.

Take a moment or two, every hour on the hour, to appraise the previous hour impartially, then set yourself the aim to use the hour yet to come even more fully than you used the previous hour.

Taking each hour as a separate unit of your life, strive to use each of these units of life with greater and greater quality.

Force yourself to find a way to make each succeeding hour more profitable for your work than the last and, at the same time, find a way to settle all your debts with the machine and with nature, up to the present moment.

To live the remainder of your life rehearsing for death, hour by hour is not a morbid fascination with death, but a method of living life more deeply.

No one can extract more from every moment of life than a terminal patient who knows more or less when he can expect to die. If we have thought deeply on the possible ways in which we can spend our last days, we change our lives radically.

If we know with certainty that we will soon die, we will bend every ounce of will available to us to the extraction from every hour remaining to us of every possible drop of quality.

This is the real meaning of the ancient Essene saying, "The Last Days are at hand." We all face Judgment not from others but our own last-minute final appraisal of our lives. We must not fail to pass this test.

Every single moment is an eternal part of Creation.

In each moment it is possible to extract a finer substance which we can call "essence of life".

On a clean sheet of paper, draw a picture which represents for you the substance "air". Now draw a picture of the substance "food". Now a picture of the substance "impressions". Finally draw a picture of the substance of "a moment".

Because these can all be pictured as substances it should give you the hint that they really *are* substances—that even moments of time are a form of matter.

If we are successful in extracting the finer substances from these more gross material substances familiar to everybody in general, then we must sooner or later pay something for them.

This is called the *Law of Equilibrium*. We must eventually pay for what we extract of life.

But to pay in the moment for our use of the moment is what we call "real doing".

In the beginning, we can only imagine what it is "to do" with the thinking, feeling or moving apparatus, but eventually, with work-experience, we find that real doing is paying in the moment, leaving nothing for the future.

It is not too late even now, although much of your life has been wasted in sleep. From today you can begin to prepare for death and at the same time increase the quality of your life with the machine.

But take this warning: do not wait too long; *maybe this one last hour is in fact all that remains to you!*

You may be able to glibly repeat this verbatim, but unless actually practiced, this cannot mean anything.

The awakened machine, functioning higher mental and emotional apparati, and radiation of one's presence are the only real tools of communication.

At the end of each hour, having completed your appraisal of the work-profit of the previous hour, imagine waking up suddenly in a completely new world in which you recognize the fact that you are a total stranger, even though everything looks vaguely familiar to you.

Establishing a whole new working relationship with this new world demonstrates clearly that your apparent automatic continuation in the flow of life is not really the same at all from hour to hour.

You could see yourself as a ghost destined to wander from world to world as an uninvited guest... From this vantage point, of what value is anything accomplished in the course of ordinary life? Consider the results of all your strivings of the past. What are they worth now?

We in the Work are in many ways dead to the world, and at the same time more alive than anything in it. Work...a small, strange difference in our lives and yet, to some of us, life is meaningless without this little difference.

It should be easy to see that life is futile in the ordinary sense. Every accomplishment, no matter how great in the scale of planetary life, sooner or later is lost in the big sense.

Time grinds every grain to dust. Even the biggest names in history sooner or later will be forgotten. To understand the real possibilities of life on Earth, we must discover what can be accomplished in this world which would be of use beyond this world.

Study the lives of those who managed to amass great wealth, armies, influence and power over others. Of what use to them, now that they are dead, are their great accomplishments? Even during life they were empty dreams.

Learn to use each hour to the fullest possible profit. Write a detailed plan for your last hour of life.

By this little exercise, you will be forced to sink your roots of mentation deeply into the whole question of the real value of life as a prisoner in the human biological machine just to understand how to die.

Not just anyone is able to really die. The human biological machine can be converted to one form of fertilizer or another for the use of organic life on the planet, but, because the Creation is eternal, we cannot really die just because the biological machine dies.

To die forever to this world is an honor which must be paid for by conscious labor and intentional suffering through the process of Conscious Eternal Return.

Picture the events, sensations, thoughts and feelings of each hour of life on Earth. Ask yourself, "Is this really what I wish to do with the last hour of my life?" If not, you must find a way to satisfy this question.

Look at life as a business in which time is money.

Time literally represents the money of life. We are given a certain amount to spend and no more when we come into this world.

Perhaps now you can see how stupidly you have spent much of it.

Even your aim in life just to relax has been defeated. As a consumer of life you have cheated yourself.

All your life you believed everything was free. Air is free, time is free. Now suddenly you discover that these are not free, that you pay dearly for the use of the machine; you pay with precious time. Every moment you are here, it costs something, one moment is the price of each breath.

How can you ever recoup these losses? If you have spent all your money on vacations, nothing is left to you now but empty nostalgia.

For years you have spent your time as if it were one continuous, endless allowance from your parents.

Only now, after the family fortune has been spent down to the last penny and you find yourself bankrupt, do you discover that you are forced to earn every hour of life. All your life you were like a child, spending time, the money of transformation, like a newlywed.

You will find many excuses not to practice the last hour of life. The will and habits of the machine are very strong, but you can learn to do more and more once you begin.

Think of your last hour of life as a great ballet for which a lifetime of continual practice is necessary.

INDEX

Conscience, 102, 123 ff.,
    178
Consciousness
    forms of, 2
    Objective, 129
    ordinary, 3
Creation, 87, 99, 111, 125,
    153 ff., 182 ff.
    Crown of, 153
    Scale of, 153
Crocodile, The, 48

Dark Night of the Soul,
102
Data, 95
    mental, 1
Descartes, 73
Dimensions, higher, 7, 41,
    86, 145, 154
Djinn, 17

Emotion(s), 26 ff., 32
    negative, 6, 24 ff.,
    43, 46, 127
Essenes, 145, 181
Essential self, 4
Eternal Return, 6, 7, 56,
    184
Evolution, 31, 41, 108, 127,
    139, 166, 179

Fields, electrical, 34
Garden of Eden, 58
Gnothe Seauton, 138

Headbrain, 12 ff., 42, 99
Heisenberg Principle, 55
Hitler, 80

Holy Planet Purgatory,
    102

Identification, 7, 30, 52,
    56, 83, 131
Impartiality, 66
Impression(s), 23, 73, 120,
    178 ff.
Inquisition, 80

Judgment, 181

Klein bottle, 154

Labyrinth, 14
Law(s)
    as higher beings, 110
    of Catching Up, 145
    of Equilibrium, 182
    of Falling, 146
    of Seven, 155
    of the octave, 116, 155
    of Three, 155
    of work-necessity, 67
Life, mechanical, 33
Luckium, 166

Machine, awakened, 9,
    38, 54, 105 ff., 127
Man on the Cross, 134
Maya, definition of, 7
Maze-brightness, 14
Meditation, 97
Mentation, 12, 97 ff., 184
Moebius strip, 154
Monasteries, 92
Monk, 134
    way of, 25

ABOUT THE AUTHOR, E.J. GOLD

E.J. Gold is a true voyager in the heroic tradition, always keeping the highest aims and the purest ethics close to his heart throughout his explorations. His life story is a veritable odyssey through contemporary society, an adventurous journey to unlock inner secrets which he learned to skillfully communicate to others.

Mr. Gold had what could only be called a "culturally privileged" childhood in the sense that his parents' New York apartment was a meeting place of the New York intelligentsia of the time who gathered with his father Horace L. Gold, founding editor of *Galaxy* (science fiction) magazine. As a young child he met visionary writers, artists and scientists. With an early penchant for writing and all the arts, he began—as a teenager—to publish science fiction stories, to write film scripts and to work with his father on *Galaxy* magazine.

A gifted painter and sculptor, Gold moved to Los Angeles in the late 50's, studied art and cinema there, and emerged in the '60's as a respected sculptor in the California Nine group. In Hollywood, he wrote scripts for movies and television shows and performed in his own right as a comedian and a dramatic actor. With a lively interest in classical and jazz music, he professionally produced and engineered records for several major artists during the lively '60's, and he sat in with many bands in New York and Los Angeles jazz clubs.

Versatile and talented as he was, E.J. Gold was not satisfied to settle into a safe niche as a successful artist. He worked to master every art and communication field he

190

could get his hands on, always using one form to complement his knowledge in another form—culminating in his impressive success in penetration of the subject of personal transformation. Beginning in the late '50's, he worked with people in group situations to research and test the entire range of approaches to transformation.

Having begun before spiritual life was big business, E.J. Gold is still, twenty-five years later, working actively in this field. He is now internationally known as an originator of contemporary processes of transformational psychology– a teacher's teacher—and as a masterful proponent of proven ancient methods of "labyrinth voyaging" and voluntary evolution. A writer's writer as well, he's a longtime member of SFWA (Science Fiction Writers of America), a master of satire and author of more than twenty books on subjects ranging from natural childbirth and conscious dying to shamanism and techniques of mystical vision.

According to colleagues, fans and reviewers of Mr. Gold's books, his latest series, beginning with *The Human Biological Machine as a Transformational Apparatus*, is his most significant contribution to date to the literature of mysticism, consciousness and meditation. His literary specialty is the practical use of long-atrophied classics, masterpieces of ideas presented with the utmost force and clarity, ideas not spun from intellectual abstraction but tested, lived and communicated from the heart.

With *Practical Work on Self* and *Visions in the Stone*, he is taking a step causing many of his students to gasp by releasing in public format—no longer as privately-issued small-group study materials—the most sensational and profound of his discoveries over twenty-five years of research on inner awakening and transformation. Closer than ever before to the pearl-beyond-price, the heart's understanding of the never-truly-lost knowledge of life's purpose, E.J. Gold invites discerning readers everywhere to sample the banquet of his new books and take whatever they can use for their own nourishment.

FOR FURTHER STUDY . . .

Books by E.J. Gold

Practical Work on Self
Visions in the Stone: Journey to the Source of Hidden Knowledge
American Book of the Dead
The Human Biological Machine as a Transformational Apparatus
Life in the Labyrinth
Creation Story Verbatim
The Lazy Man's Guide to Death & Dying
The Invocation of Presence
Secret Talks on Voluntary Evolution
The Joy of Sacrifice

Books by Other Authors

Self-Completion: Keys to the Meaningful Life by Robert S. de Ropp
The Dream Assembly by Zalman Schachter-Shalomi
Living God Blues by Lee Lozowick
The Golden Buddha Changing Masks: Essays on
*   the Spiritual Dimension of Acting by Mark Olsen*

Talk of the Month

A journal of work ideas featuring transcriptions of lectures by
E.J. Gold. For subscription and back issue information write to
Gateways.

Spoken Word Audio

Inner Awakening and Transformation
The Rembrandt Tape
The Cogitate Tape by John Lilly, M.D., and E.J. Gold

Music from E.J. Gold, the Hi-Tech Shaman

Shaman Ritual I: 'Way Beyond the Veil
Shaman Ritual II: Golden Age
Mystical Journey of the Hi-Tech Shaman
Live at the Philharmonic I
Live at the Philharmonic II
The Cogitate Tape
Adventures of the Hi-Tech Shaman
How I Raised Myself from the Dead
Journey Through the Great Mother
Dance of the Hi-Tech Shaman
Bardo Dreams
Venus Rising

Music by Other Gateways Recording Artists

Life in the Labyrinth by Jimmi Accardi
The Wheel by Martin Silverwolf
*Where You Are by Drew Kristel and the Not Always
   North American Drum Core*

Video

The Movements Series
G. en Amerique
Hooray for Hollywood
Revenge of the Fly
Godfan
An Evening Shot to Hell with Parker Dixon

Dear Reader of *Practical Work on Self:*

This book is a manual for your use, self-contained and self-explanatory.

It can also be a gateway, the threshold to a great inner adventure. If you are one of those readers who not only reads the exercises but also applies them to gather your own experimental results—you may be ready for further volumes in the series.

Apart from the study materials listed, there is an extensive series of private publications that provide further background and an advanced course of preparation for the Work.

For a current catalog, a listing of private publications, or further information on setting up a program of preparatory work, contact Gateways at this address:

Gateways Books & Tapes
PO Box 370-PW
Nevada City, CA 95959

Tel: (530) 272-0180
Fax: (530) 272-0184
Orders: (800) 869-0658
email: info@gatewaysbooksandtapes.com